WAR IS MAKING US POOR!

Militarism Is Destroying the U.S.

by

John Rachel

Published by
Literary Vagabond Books
Los Angeles • Osaka

literaryvagabond.com

ISBN #979-8-883-94613-3

Table of Contents

Special Introduction

by Cynthia McKinney

U.S. Homeless Live on the Street (paine.tv)

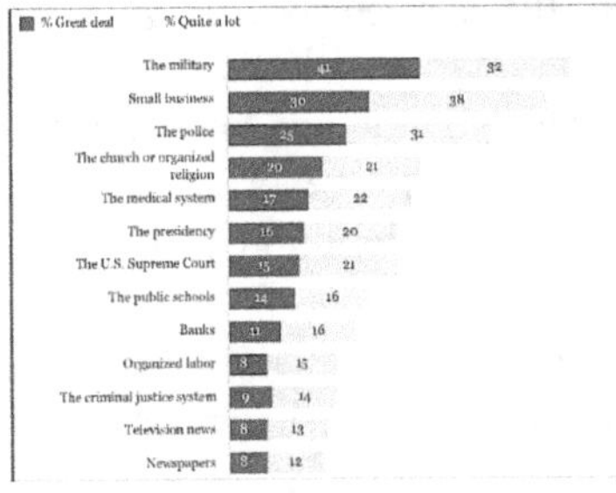

Confidence in U.S. Institutions

Belief in God Takes a Nosedive in the U.S.

As someone born and raised in the United States of America, and especially by being a "Child of the South" and a "Daughter of the Civil Rights Movement," I have seen great upheaval as well as great change in the United States. The upheaval occurred everywhere around me; and, as a Boomer, I was raised by members of the so-called Greatest Generation who deeply believed in the United States, the U.S. Constitution, and the future. My parents instilled in me the belief that success was possible with hard work, and that, as an African American in the U.S., that I could work twice as hard and get half as far, but that I could become successful, nonetheless. Vestiges of Jim Crow were all around me — and the denial that robbed the majority of my fellow countrymen the opportunity to excel and make a smooth transition into the very embodiment of the U.S. Bill of Rights that all proclaimed as desirable. So, as a result, everyone in my environment was hard working and believed in the future of the U.S., recognizing that the U.S. was a long way from a reality that was embodied in the first ten amendments to the U.S. Constitution. But, because people believed in those words, there was struggle and there was hope.

I grew up with hope. I believed. And, at the same time, I also understood that "the real U.S." was a long way from our aspirational U.S. And, concomitantly, the very real successes of the U.S. Civil Rights Movement demonstrated to me that positive change is possible. My father was in the military during WWII and served overseas. But, on his way home to Georgia after fighting for Europe's "freedom," after landing in New York City, he took the train home and he could see the stark difference between North and South USA. And, when the train reached South Carolina, he looked from his railroad car window and saw the water fountains in the train station were labeled "White" and "Colored." He disembarked the train and made a bee line straight for the "White" water fountain. Of course, despite still being in his U.S. Army uniform coming from the theatre of war being fought for "freedom" and "democracy," my father was arrested. Somehow, he knew a young lawyer in Florida, Alcee Hastings, who made the trip to South Carolina to bail my father out of jail. Decades later, I served in the U.S. Congress with Alcee Hastings, who became a Member of Congress from Florida. Yes, I have witnessed great change in the U.S. — positive change. My own life infused me with the recognition that positive change was possible and that recognition gave me a reasonable foundation for hope. I do believe that my experiences were of the sort that an entire generation shared, especially in the South where the Civil Rights Movement caused great personal introspection on the part of many in the "White" population. Whites in the North were smug in their self- assuredness that they were so much better than their compatriots in the South and therefore, they had no need for introspection or change.

But, somehow, the U.S. came to be dominated, not by leaders who sought to make life better for the people of the U.S., not by leadership that sought to deepen the liberties guaranteed in the U.S. Constitution, but instead, sought to subvert those liberties while no one was watching them. So, a smokescreen was created that distracted the optimisms of my youth from succeeding generations and somehow, the U.S. and its people took a deep turn away from constitutionalism and liberty. Goals were changed, values were subverted, and ideas as distractions became pervasive. The monied interests were not interested in spreading freedom across the land; their interests were more private, personal, and pecuniary. They created new leaders for the people whose silver tongues, embellished with unlimited Federal Reserve Notes, made people in the U.S. believe that a new leadership was better than the authentic leadership that rose from the problems and successes of grassroots people. Unfortunately, while the lived reality of people in the U.S. began to take a nosedive in terms of U.S. policy outcomes, the rhetoricians triumphed. So much so that when Donald Trump was sworn into the U.S. Presidency, he announced that he was going to appoint billionaires to his Cabinet and his explanation was that they knew what success was. (And I thought to myself, "Behind every great fortune is a great crime.")

As a result of my many publicly-voiced divergences from the monied rhetoricians and their backers squatting in U.S. public spaces, tolerance for my opinions was obliterated and I was expelled from politics as a whole in the U.S., the U.S. Congress (by way of two stolen elections, one with and one without the use of electronic voting machines), and censored or shadow-banned out of social media attention. I was deplatformed before deplatforming became a badge of honor. And I am not alone in that, because many, many others suffered my fate, privately. I just suffered it publicly. And, in the end, I found life, happiness, and a place outside of the U.S. And, when I return to the U.S. to visit my friends and family, more and more it seems unrecognizable to me.

State power is now firmly in the hands of the monied interests and no wonder I see hopelessness, poverty, and anger on the U.S. streets. And, the U.S. has been at war against some innocent population every year of my adulthood. The U.S. is bombing innocent people today and putting authentic leaders, like Pakistan's Imran Khan, in prison while installing known kleptocrats in positions of authority all over the world. They have done to the United States what the people of the U.S. allowed them to do to other countries around the world. Donald Trump characterized some countries as "sh*thole countries." It is important to note the role of U.S. policy in the creation of such a type of country and because those negative forces were permitted by the people of the U.S., now, the U.S. has clearly become one of those types of countries, too.

Life expectancy in the U.S. is declining despite the increasing amount of money spent on health care in the U.S. Homelessness is on display across the country. Disease is rampant, drug abuse is pervasive, and hopelessness in the U.S. is endemic. But, because of these conditions, some people are waking up to the possibilities that real solutions present, instead of the nostrums of the rhetoricians. The problem is that we don't yet have critical mass of those whose eyes are opened — with many preferring the snake oil of the "woke."

Therefore, I have just formulated that, were I to run again for U.S. Congress, my H.R. 1 would be Repeal of the Federal Reserve Act of 1913; my H.R. 2 would amend the National Security Act of 1947; and my H.R. 3 would repeal the Homeland Security Act of 2002. I'm hoping that someone will see this and run with this as their platform, thus saving me from doing it! :-)

Dr. Martin Luther King, Jr. and his wife Coretta, spoke often about the "revolution of values" that was needed in the U.S. We need a revolution, alright, but what we got was the revolution of values of those who work on behalf of the international bankster class. We've had lots of change — the kind of change that hurts too many people, that concentrates

power too much. I do believe that these three legislative initiatives could catalyze the kind of change that people in the U.S. desperately need.

Nothing short of a complete disruption of "business as usual" in the U.S. can put the U.S. on the right track. Anything else would be an "eyewash" as my students say, just the art of putting new lipstick on the same ol' pig.

Cynthia McKinney is an American politician and assistant professor at North South University, Bangladesh. As a member of the Democratic Party, she served six terms in the United States House of Representatives, as the first African American woman ever elected to represent Georgia. She was also the first Member of Congress to demand an investigation of the events of 9/11 and the first to file articles of impeachment against George W. Bush. She voted against every war-funding bill put before her. In 2008, Cynthia McKinney won the Green Party nomination and ran for U.S. President.

Foreword

by three distinguished thought leaders.

LT. COL. WILLIAM ASTORE

Recently, I was reading the letters of Thomas Henry Huxley, who made a wise assertion in 1888: "Battles, like hypotheses, are not to be multiplied beyond necessity." My country, the United States of America, has been needlessly multiplying its battles around the world without necessity. The result has been a series of devastating wars in places like Vietnam, Iraq, and Afghanistan, wars that killed millions for little purpose other than the enrichment of what President Dwight D. Eisenhower in 1961 termed the military-industrial complex. Thus, Martin Luther King Jr. was right to conclude in 1967 that the United States had become the greatest purveyor of violence on the planet, its unbridled pursuit of militarism producing a form of spiritual death.

As James Madison, one of America's founders, wrote near the close of the eighteenth century, no nation can preserve its freedom and maintain a healthy democracy when it embraces and pursues endless warfare. John Rachel knows this, feels this, and embraces the challenge of fighting against it. He knows America is dedicating more than half of its federal discretionary spending to wars, as the Pentagon budget soars toward $900 billion in 2024. He knows America is suffering from a form of spiritual death. He knows militarism will be the death, not only of democracy in America, but possibly of our planet itself, whether in quick time due to global nuclear war or in slow motion due to war-driven calamities aggravated by climate change.

America needs to change course. It needs to learn the word "peace" again. It needs to embrace diplomacy and reject militarism. It needs to stop being the world's greatest purveyor of violence. It needs to dismantle its global network of 800 military bases, it needs to reject its vision of "full-spectrum dominance," it needs to end its glorification of warriors and warfighters as heroes, it needs to stop exporting weapons to the world's worst hotspots. But how?

As I write this, the U.S. government is sending massive arms shipments to Israel to enable ethnic cleansing in Gaza. Palestinian innocents, including thousands of women and children, are being pummeled and eviscerated by bombs and missiles carrying the label, "Made in USA." America, which fancies itself a beacon of freedom, has become an abattoir of death through endless war.

I served in the U.S. military for twenty years. I taught thousands of military cadets the lessons of history. Yet I failed to question and challenge the system in meaningful ways until after I retired from the military. Somehow, collectively, Americans need to find the courage to change our violent ways. We need to act—now.

John Rachel's book, by provoking us to think and to examine our often-unquestioned biases and assumptions, is just what we need to execute an "about-face" in America's constant march to war.

William J. Astore is a retired lieutenant colonel (USAF) and professor of history, and is a senior fellow at the Eisenhower Media Network (EMN), an organization of critical veteran military and national security professionals. He has taught at the Air Force Academy and Naval Postgraduate School, and now teaches history at the Pennsylvania College of Technology. He is the author or co-author of three books and numerous articles focusing on military history as well as the history of science, technology, and religion.

His personal blog is Bracing Views [https://bracingviews.com/].

MATTHEW HOH

The costs of US wars and militarism are obscene, dangerous and insidious. Across the globe, tens of millions of lives have been wrecked by death, physical and mental harm, and displacement by US invasions, occupations, airstrikes and proxy wars. Untold numbers of families and communities, both overseas and in the US, have been ruined by conflict and instability. At the same time, the opportunity costs of the trillions spent on war only offer questions about what might otherwise have been done with the $8 trillion spent on wars and another $8 trillion spent on the Pentagon's overhead just since 2001.

It is not as if these costs were worthwhile, except maybe for the military-industrial complex and its friends on Wall Street, in the media studios, in the boardrooms of fossil fuel giants, and, of course, in the halls of Congress and the White House. American imperial war-making and a militarized foreign policy have not resulted in a safer American public, stronger alliances and a more stable international community, but rather the very opposite of those things. Today, we are witnessing genocide in Palestine, the worst conventional war since World War II in Europe, conflict and terror throughout much of Africa, and tensions in East Asia that risk the nuclear third world war we, as humans, have lived in captive fear of for nearly 80 years. The threat to the American people, whether from terror attacks, getting drawn into another Middle East or European war, or from an existential nuclear war, is higher than any of us have ever known.

Not to be dismissed either is the corrosive rot that grows consistently within our society from our elected leaders' prioritization of weapons and war. The failure to invest in our people, our communities, our education, our healthcare, our infrastructure and our environment, at best, leads to a stunted and underperforming workforce and a declining quality of life. Much more likely are degrees of societal collapse as a sicker, less educated and poorer American public, burdened with decrepit infrastructure and a hollow economy, is confronted by not just its own failings and other nations that have wisely invested in themselves but a planet undone by climate change.

This last warning does not have to come to reality, but only if we understand what war and militarism have delivered us, what they further offer us, and if we follow the lead of people like John Rachel for a sane, peaceful and prosperous world.

Matthew Hoh is currently Associate Director at the Eisenhower Media Network. He has been a Senior Fellow with the Center for International Policy since 2010. Previously he served nearly twelve years with the US military in the United States Marine Corps, as well as the Department of Defense and State Department. In 2009, Matthew resigned in protest from his post in Afghanistan with the State Department over the American escalation of the war. Prior to his assignment in Afghanistan, Matthew took part in the American occupation of Iraq, with a State Department reconstruction and governance team and in 2006-2007 as a Marine Corps company commander. When not deployed, Matthew worked on Afghanistan and Iraq war policy and operations issues at the Pentagon and State Department.

Matthew's writings have appeared in online and print periodicals such as the Atlanta Journal Constitution, Defense News, the Guardian, the Huffington Post, USA Today, the Wall Street Journal and the Washington Post. He has been a guest on hundreds of news programs on radio and television. The Council on Foreign Relations has cited Matthew's resignation letter from his post in Afghanistan as an Essential Document. In 2010, Matthew was named the Ridenhour Prize Recipient for Truth Telling and, in 2021, he was awarded as a Defender of Liberty by the Committee for the Republic.

Matthew is a member of the Board of Directors for the Institute for Public Accuracy, an Advisory Board Member for the Committee to Defend Julian Assange and Civil Liberties, Expose Facts, North Carolina Committee to Investigate Torture, The Resistance Center for Peace and Justice, Veterans For Peace, and World Beyond War, and he is an Associate Member of Veteran Intelligence Professionals for Sanity (VIPS). He is a 100% disabled veteran and has been certified by North Carolina as a Peer Support Specialist for Mental Health and Substance Use Disorder.

Matthew's incisive commentary can be found at the Eisenhower Media Network [https://eisenhowermedianetwork.org/staff/matthew-hoh/], *at his personal website* [https://matthewhoh.com/], *and on* X (formerly Twitter), [@MatthewPHoh].

DAN KOVALIK

As this book by John Rachel makes is abundantly clear, war is killing us, literally!

According to the Watson Institute for International and Public Affairs at Brown University, the death toll from just the "war on terror" which began in 2001 has been astounding. Thus, the Watson Institute explains[1] that:

- Over 940,000 people have died in the post-9/11 wars due to direct war violence.
- An estimated 3.6-3.8 million people have died indirectly in post-9/11 war zones, bringing the total death toll to at least 4.5-4.7 million and counting.
- Over 432,000 civilians have been killed as a result of the fighting.

In addition, 38 million people have been displaced by this war.

The Watson Institute further notes that this war has cost an incredible $8 trillion. And of course, this is money that could have gone, instead of to killing, to saving lives. Can one imagine if that $8 trillion had been applied toward relieving hunger, disease, homelessness and drug addiction, and toward needed infrastructure as well as protecting the environment? It is heartbreaking to even contemplate this. What a world we might have today had we put such resources towards creation instead of destruction.

But this is not what happened. Instead, our government, often in direct contradiction of the will of the American people who, as polls have shown, largely opposed war and huge military expenditures, decided to spend the past quarter of a century waging war on huge swaths of the world. And, instead of making the world safer, these wars have only destabilized the world further and led to more war, more suffering and more terror. While the defense industry made trillions, the rest of us lost and humanity has been placed in an ever more precarious position.

Rachel's book is a wake-up call to radically change our nation's priorities. Even as I write these words, the Biden Administration is seeking a record military budget for 2024 in the amount of nearly $900 billion[2] and is poised to expand a regional war in the Middle East. Meanwhile, homelessness, drug abuse and despair grow in our nation's cities.

This madness must end, and it must end now before it is too late.

Dan Kovalik is the author of critically-acclaimed No More War: How the West Violates International Law by Using 'Humanitarian' Intervention to Advance Economic and Strategic Interests, The Plot to Scapegoat Russia, The Plot to Attack Iran, The Plot to Overthrow Venezuela, *and* The Plot to Control the World, *among many other equally important works. His most recent book is* The Case for Palestine: Why It Matters and Why You Should Care. *He is a dedicated peace activist and has been a labor and human rights lawyer since graduating from Columbia Law School in 1993. He has represented plaintiffs in ATS cases arising out of egregious human rights abuses in South America. He received the David W. Mills Mentoring Fellowship from Stanford Law School and has lectured throughout the world. He is accessible on* X (formerly Twitter) [@danielmkovalik].

Author's Introduction

When I decided to write this book, understandably I was concerned that the necessary facts to construct a solid case would not be readily available. After all, the autocratic ruling elites who are in fact running the country, aided by their lapdog stenographic media puppets, do everything in their power to create false optimism, manufacture hope out of thin air, prop up the faith and trust of everyday citizens in our government and our economic institutions, unhesitatingly censoring the facts and promoting fanciful fictions. We are 24/7 barraged with provably false narratives, immersed in fairy tales, and subjected to crass manipulation of reality.

However, it turned out I had no need to worry. The incompetence, negligence, abuse of power, outright fraud and corruption, are so pervasive and abundant, the evidence constitutes orchards of low hanging fruit. Discovering the ugly truth is purely a matter of doing some focused research.

If the impact of the calculated deceptions on us regular folks weren't so devastating, we might find our bumbling public officials hysterically funny. What a belly-buckling barrel of laughs it is when Secretary of the Treasury Janet Yellen appears at a press conference to report how splendid things are, how superbly our economy is performing, how ominous signs of collapse are minor hiccups, anomalous and fleeting. Or when Secretary of State Anthony Blinken stares into the camera with his trademark, vacant, believability-demolishing, puppy-dog-lost-his-favorite-bone brown eyes, explaining what a fantastic investment the $113 billion we've sent to Ukraine[1] is, how wonderfully things are going to turn out, with peace and democracy and love breaking out all over the planet as a result of the blood-drenched war we started there. Or when Kamala Harris tries to say anything that makes sense. Or Joe Biden? Ha ha ha. A feeble, old clown with dementia and a big mouth is just a bucket load of knee-slapping hilarity.

Unfortunately, none of the idiocy and prevarication is funny in the least. In fact, it's about as tragic as it can get; with thousands of corpses littering the globe; more conflict, violence and human suffering, both globally and domestically, than we can keep track of; the prospects of World War III and potential nuclear annihilation growing more ominous and likely every day; our national debt completely out of control, our economy staring into an abyss; trust in the U.S. and its leadership at an all-time low, both at home and globally; by every measure, the quality of life in America for the vast majority of citizens in rapid decline; and finally, hopes for improvement of any of this, becoming more and more the product of wishful thinking and hallucinatory drugs.

Let me cut directly to the chase: I firmly believe that most of this, meaning the accelerating dysfunction of America as a society and nation, and the resulting collapse in the quality of life of its citizens, is attributable to the U.S. obsession with war, military conquest, and empire building.

Granted, nothing is really quite that simple, but the focus on endless war and excessive militarism provides a good place to start focusing our attention.

The reasons are obvious. We'll get into the details later, but here in broad strokes are the two decisive factors.

First, the largest portion of the discretionary budget of the federal government is spent on defense. The "indiscretion" of dumping all that money into the military creates debilitating shortages of investment across the board in every other sector of our society. The preponderance of what the vast majority of citizens do and experience trying to live meaningful and productive lives has nothing to do with war and supposedly defending our borders. Their needs and the conditions for them as non-combatants to function and thrive are grossly neglected when most of the federal budget feeds the insatiable appetite of the war machine. Moreover, it's not just the billions of dollars in absolute numbers which smothers the rest of the economy. Investment is a multiplier. Investing in non-military enterprises and institutions multiplies their positive impact on the overall fruitfulness of society and the individual lives of the citizenry. Better education, better training, safer streets, efficient and effective health care, safe food, air and water – the list goes on and on – means a more productive, happier, more mentally and physically fit population. It means an economy, institutions, and communities which work well and "promote the general welfare". Which in turn generates more of the same. What does preparation for war, conflict, confrontation, destruction, death, and fear of the "enemy" multiply? It's little wonder that we average more than one mass shooting every day. It's little wonder we have so many angry, homeless, undernourished, unemployed, underemployed, discouraged, and cynical people in this country. Living in fear, missing any healthy connection with one another or their communities, lacking the basic necessities, and certainly without the backstop of an adequate safety net to help deal with emergencies, equates to a population which is always scrambling, ever anxious, often just barely surviving, or at bare minimum, facing unnecessary and troubling obstacles to having a decent life. Such shortcomings breed frustration, hopelessness, cynicism and ultimately rage. Perpetual war and excessive militarism void the promises intrinsic to the American Dream and referenced in the Constitution. Tolerating, or more accurately, promoting misery and despair with skewed priorities, is an insult to the framers of that document who clearly had much higher hopes for our nation.

Second, because of the excesses of militarization and empire building, we have transitioned into a permanent war economy. By either design or stupidity, we squandered the enormous manufacturing/consumer economic power base we had created after World War II, ceded the critical advantages of an economy which had depth and diversity. For what? To build weapons and become the biggest merchant of death on the planet. Here again, investment is the multiplier. We stopped investing in workers, in citizens, in our schools and communities – noting that in a sane and civilized society this is just as much the responsibility of the private sector as the public – and built the war machine that now drives and sustains the decaying shell of our economy. And hand-in-hand with this transformation has been financialization and pervasive, wanton, reckless and ultimately self-sabotaging, de-industrialization. Of course, these processes are the direct result of inverted priorities which put profits before people – that rob the poor to enrich the already wealthy. A war economy epitomizes this. Human life and quality living are devalued and deprioritized. Humans are cogs in the war machine or cannon fodder on the battlefield.

This evisceration of the American Dream by an out-of-control military was anticipated by President Dwight D. Eisenhower. He sounded the alarm in his farewell address as president in 1961:

> "In the councils of government, we must guard against the acquisition of unwarranted influence, whether sought or unsought, by the military-industrial complex. The potential for the disastrous rise of misplaced power exists and will persist."

We are now experiencing the realization of President Eisenhower's ominous warning: the transformation of our entire society, the corporate capture of our economy and government institutions, the marginalization of our individual values, the inversion of our national priorities, and the razing of our democracy. This self-sabotaging lunacy is driven by a combination of ravenous profit-seeking by the military-industrial complex (MIC), and the imperial ambitions of a cabal of delusional sociopaths at the power centers of the Deep State, who have, without ever consulting the people, decided the U.S. is chosen by destiny to rule the entire world.

The impact of this military madness is far-reaching and bottomless.

It eventually bodes the total impoverishment of the U.S. as a nation – economically, socially, morally, spiritually – and the complete bankrupting of America and its citizens.

Yes, folks ... WAR IS MAKING US POOR!

This is not just a clever meme. Because with deadly accuracy, it identifies and indicts the central cause of the atrophy, decline, degeneration, the systemic sickness which is destroying our country. This viral pathogen shows no sign of abating. In fact, it is accelerating. This book will look at where exactly we are at in the advancing stages of this destructive pathology. The sincere hope is that people will wake up and put an end to this insanity before it puts an end to us.

• • •

Now let me briefly explain the organization of this book.
I'm going from the macro to the micro.
We'll proceed top to bottom.
This only makes sense. Because the decisions made and the policies instituted which are bankrupting us as a society and, in the final analysis, us as individual citizens, have been a top-down exercise. Likewise, the real-world looting and squandering of our national wealth, are implemented by and serve the exclusive interests of those at the top, at the expense of those at the bottom – or more accurately, everyone below those at the very top.

Top-down. Hierarchical control and abuse of power. It's hardly a secret which way the money flows. Like a vertical tsunami, it continues to migrate upwards[2] to the stratospheric upper reaches of the ultra-wealthy. Even during the Covid-19 crisis, when millions lost their jobs, tens of thousands of medium and small businesses went bankrupt, and the government forked out billions of dollars to keep families afloat, billionaires in the U.S. increased their wealth by almost $1 trillion.[3] Along with such vast piles of lucre, goes even more power to leverage and accelerate that upward flow of money and power.

The first and most effective platform for this massive heist is the federal government. So we'll start there. Then we'll work our way down the hierarchy of official power. Next state and municipal government. Finally, we'll look at how all of this impacts real people living real lives.

Each level exhibits unequivocally the appalling havoc produced by a financialized, de-industrialized, war economy: The shortage of funds; the astronomical debt carried by government institutions, businesses, banks, and individual citizens; the galling deficiencies in the quality of services; the trap of ever-shrinking options and fading opportunities for personal growth and improvement; the cannibalism of our money supply and potential future investment, both public and private, by interest on debt. To make matters worse, the chaos of a disintegrating economic/political framework has created the perceived need for increasing totalitarian control: the iron fist of military-style law enforcement, the complete control of the "narrative" such that we are awash in lies and pure propaganda, the exponential increase in surveillance and tracking, the monitoring of our movement, our communications, our transactions, our ideological leanings, our loyalties and associations. We are increasingly living in a police state, which more and more resembles what we used to mock and vilify in countries like Stasi East Germany and the USSR. It is totalitarianism with American characteristics –

Sheldon Wolin called it inverted totalitarianism[4] – but in the end no less oppressive and anti-democratic than any other top-down tyranny.

Note that as we work our way down through the ranks, the amount of leverage – the power to influence and reshape policy to try to fix the mess – diminishes. This is how hierarchical systems can end up being the officially sanctioned mechanism for victimizing those on the bottom. It's "trickle down". Trickle down hopelessness.

Theoretically, it shouldn't be this way. Theoretically, we are a democratic nation. Theoretically, we the people should have a voice in the direction and functioning of the nation. The unspoken truth is, we have never strictly had true representative democracy, thus everyday citizens have always been lacking a decisive say in running the country. But at one time, we regular folks at least had some power. This is no longer the case.[5] While, for example, in the 1930s, late 60s and early 70s, we could pose enough of a threat, those in power took notice. Out of fear they would accommodate some of the demands of the middle and working classes, making adjustments to official policy such as to prevent unmanageable levels of discontent and a possible insurrection. Now, however, the ruling class operates behind an impregnable firewall. They don't see us, they don't hear us, and they certainly don't care about us.

The current rigged system is the result. More riches for the rich, less of everything for the rest of us. We end up impoverished and powerless. We fight wars we never agreed to fight, buy billions of dollars of military junk we don't need, blanket the globe with bases so we can be the policeman of the world – all colossal waste we never voted for. We even pay to rebuild other countries destroyed by U.S. military aggression, while our own infrastructure goes to ruin. On and on. We'll see that this mounts up to trillions and trillions of dollars.

Everyday citizens would NEVER introduce and subject our economy and federal budgeting to the perverse agenda we now have in place. If everyday citizens were not barraged constantly by lies and propaganda and they truly understood what is going on, they would reject in the blink of an eye the current economic model in its entirely.

I'll take it a step further.

If everyday citizens had any idea how wantonly and ruthlessly they're being abused and exploited, I have no doubt we'd see a ten-million-man lynch mob march on Washington DC and there would be a revolution in this country! The people have been scammed, conned, and brainwashed into believing this is how things must work, that it's the best world for all parties involved. This is pure fabrication by the power elites at the top, who maintain control of all the necessary levers of government, and own and control a media which keeps most of the citizenry distracted, confused, misinformed, dazed and deluded.

For us to fully understand what must come next, if anything resembling a democratic nation and properly functioning society is to reestablish itself out of the dysfunction we now find ourselves in, it's vital as we proceed here to keep in mind that even at the highest levels of government, what happens impacts every single person *individually* … as individual human beings living their lives day-to-day, attempting to piece together a decent existence, maintain a household, shape a neighborhood and a community which supports them and contributes to their own and the health and happiness of those around them – family, friends, neighbors, fellow citizens. We are all in this business of life together. It's fundamentally impossible to separate the individual from the whole. And we can't separate "big government" from the "little guy", somehow believing they are unconnected and coexisting in parallel worlds.

Which means that every shortfall, every budget downsizing and shortcut by governing bodies, and even the well-meaning deficit budgeting which "kicks the can down the road", are not mere abstract numbers on a spreadsheet. Every compromise of sensible and wholesome financing for government programs delivering some service or protection, either now or sometime in the future, directly impacts *people*: i.e. everyday folks, citizens young and old. Every deficit, every wasted dollar, every government program canceled because of lack of funding, every unjustified, irresponsible tax cut or giveaway subsidy, means something real and unfortunate on the ground: poor quality education; inferior health care, lack of access to health care; poor or no public transportation; neighborhoods where it's not safe to walk down the street or for kids to make the short trip to school; unhealthy and polluted water and air; potholes, sewer rats, stray dogs; drug dealers and addicts; homeless people; urban blight turning whole swaths of our cities into war zones, policed by militarized cops who look like they're on combat missions in Ukraine; on and on. Those "negative numbers" on a spread sheet equate to an abuse and ruination of *real people!* Those "metrics" equate to depriving individuals of the support, encouragement, and nurturing which are fundamental to a healthy, humane, holistically functioning society.

Again, referring specifically to spending on war, we look to the profound words of Dwight D. Eisenhower:

> "Every gun that is made, every warship launched, every rocket fired signifies, in the final sense a theft from those who hunger and are not fed, those who are cold and are not clothed. This world in arms is not spending money alone. It is spending the sweat of its laborers, the genius of its scientists, the hopes of its children."

We can apply this same humanistic logic to all government waste and recklessness. Current priorities and policies are a formula for societal failure.

It's probably impossible to come up with exact dollar numbers for the negative impact of institutional negligence on each person. But recognize that the numbers are real, not abstract budgetary figures. Bankrupt government bankrupts each and every citizen individually, stealing from both their present and their future.

I can't state this forcefully enough: We must keep the irrefutable fact of *personal willful negligence* – a failure of epic proportions by government – first and foremost in mind as we now turn to the tragic state of our economy, the enormous disservice that it represents in the lives of our citizens, and if left uncorrected, the bleak prospects it portends for the future of our nation.

Along the way we will draw some actionable lessons about what causes and perpetuates the ongoing impoverishment of the vast majority of U.S. citizens, good, decent folks who have for too long been hypnotized and conned by the myth of the American Dream – a dream that now looks like a war movie.

Numbers of Scale

The other day on TikTok, I saw one of the most astonishingly idiotic postings I've ever encountered, since I began my love-hate relationship with social media almost twenty years ago. Do you remember the intoxicating early days of Myspace? Yes, I was there too. Back then, I couldn't imagine such a mass phenomenon become even more puerile. I was so wrong.

Anyway, here's what the TikToker said . . .

> *Elon Musk has $148 billion. If he gave a billion dollars each to all 8 billion people on the planet, he'd still have $140 billion.*

You have to wonder. Is this guy actually that arithmetically challenged? Apparently he is. Then you have to ask, how common is this?

I prefer to believe that such a level of stupidity is uncommon.

At the same time, such an extreme and ridiculous example does point to a very common difficulty we all to a great degree confront. That is the inability to grasp numbers of enormous scale, to achieve the same level of immediate cognition as we do smaller numbers. We hear 'dozen' and we instantaneously "see" – as in our mind's eye – twelve of whatever it is. But huge numbers?

This noteworthy impairment is more pervasive than we prefer to think.

I've often heard it said about human mortality – and I fully agree – that one death is a tragedy, but a million deaths is a statistic. I think I speak for most of us when I say it's impossible to wrap our heads around the piles of corpses which clog human history. Up to 50,000,000 died in Europe, Asia, North Africa, and Arabia during the Black Plague; 15-22,000,000 killed in WWI; 75,000,000 deaths from WWII; 6,000,000 Jews killed in the Holocaust; 27,000,000 Soviet citizens vanquished fighting the Nazis; up to 50,000,000 died in the Great Chinese Famine 1959-1961. Speaking of which ...

I'm still constantly stupefied by *this* horrifying "statistic", an ugly truth relentlessly unfolding in the midst of today's incredible abundance, despite our sophisticated and highly advanced science, industry, and agriculture. Here it is:

24,000 people die EVERY SINGLE DAY of starvation. EVERY DAY!

I can't begin to imagine that today, scattered across the globe, are thousands of barely breathing skeletal human beings whose hearts will stop beating because they couldn't dig up a worm or a plant root to eat. Where are these pathetic souls dying? An old man in a metal shed in a Lagos, Nigeria ghetto? Some child in the tattered tent of desert nomads in Rajasthan? Some family migrating from Syria, camped on the side of the road in Bulgaria? Or closer to home, a baby tossed in a dumpster by a crack mama in Harlem? A homeless man in Portland, Oregon who days on end couldn't find enough edible garbage in the trash containers of McDonald's to stay alive? 24,000 shriveled, shrunken souls in 24,000 places somewhere here on Earth, exhaling their last breaths as their bodies surrender to the bottomless void of hunger. EVERY DAY!

And if by some miracle and the assistance of AI, I were able to identify *all* 24,000 of today's victims of starvation, I'd have to start all over tomorrow. And the day after that.

Maybe it's a protective mechanism to not be able to grasp so much human misery. One death is a tragedy. A million deaths ... a number in a notebook, on computer screen or a spreadsheet.

This math myopia applies across the board. I take an extra plastic bag at the supermarket[1] to keep the apples and kiwis separate. 2 billion people make a similar choice this week. Pretty soon we have the oceans glutted with plastics and microplastics. The sea currents swirl and eddy, the bags and bottles float and drift forming long tendrils and majestic roiling waves of unrecycled, plastic garbage. Eventually, almost as if guided by some invisible hand, a portion of it, seeking its own company, coalesces in the middle of the Pacific Ocean, forming an island of enduring human detritus twice the size of Texas.[2]

It all starts so innocently. I just wanted to keep my apples and kiwis separate. I'm not sure why. Maybe because the person ahead of me in line kept their cucumbers and bell peppers separate?

There's a point to this rambling tale. And this is it: as powerful and sophisticated as our gray matter is, as stunning and creative as we are as a species, when any phenomenon or entity is scaled up in quantity or frequency, there comes a point where it is *recorded* in our consciousness, but *not fully appreciated, not thoroughly and absolutely grasped.* A point where it becomes remote or abstract and we are incapable of fully connecting with it – viscerally? emotionally? empathically? Intangibility and disconnect set in.

Which brings us to . . .

Big Money

I'm old enough to remember the 1950s television show, *The Millionaire*. As the Wikipedia article explains[1]: "It told the stories of people who were given one million dollars ($10.9 million in 2022 dollars) from a benefactor who insisted they must never know his identity …"

It almost seems quaint in this day of billionaires – with hyperventilating talking heads beside themselves speculating about who will be the first *trillionaire* – to be talking about such a paltry sum.

But have you ever seen a million dollars?

Here's what it looks like.

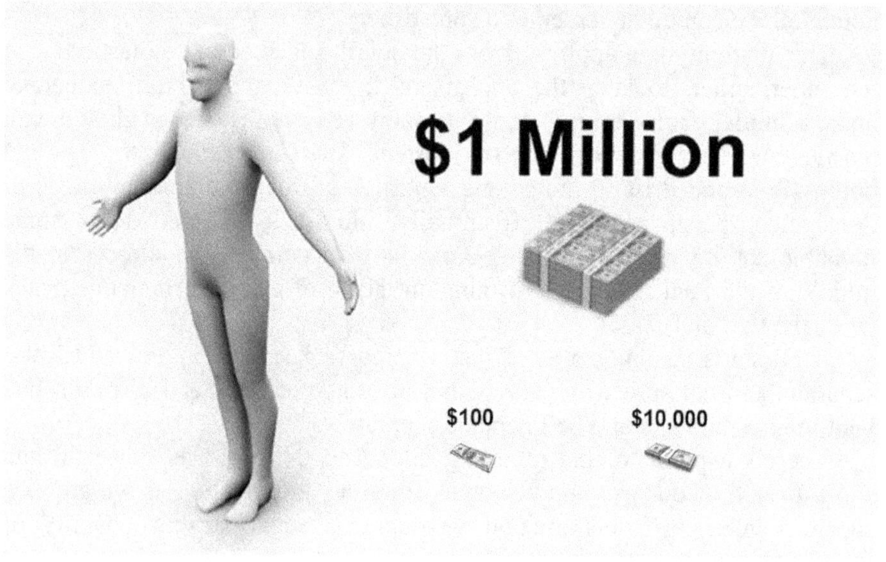

Does that help?

Apparently, just like in the movies, $1,000,000 in $100 bills would fit in a suitcase. For sure, it would certainly buy a lot of Happy Meals. Or lip gloss. Or designer t-shirts. Or perhaps life-saving surgery for a loved one.

No matter how you dice it, a million dollars is a lot of money, even today. For the many Americans who couldn't come up with $400 cash for an emergency,[2] it's a stratospheric sum.

At the same time, it's not. It entirely depends on context and perspective.

Try to wrap your head around this.

Bloomberg News recently reported[3] that for the first six months of 2023, Elon Musk increased his net worth by $96.6 billion and Mark Zuckerberg increased his by $58.9 billion. For Elon Musk this equates to his making $21,994,536 per hour, every hour, 24 hours a day, seven days a week.

Let that sink in. Elon Musk made almost $22 million per hour ... *even while he was sleeping!*

Mark Zuckerberg earned a more modest $13,410,747 per hour, every hour, 24/7 for the same six months. Not even 2/3^{rds} of what Musk made. Should we feel sorry for him? Maybe round up some donations at Go Fund Me?

A few years ago, I did similar calculations for Jeff Bezos. It turned out that he could have given every single one of his employees a $10 per hour raise, and still made over $11,000,000 per hour for himself – *every hour on the hour*, another $11,000,000+. Of course, instead of giving raises, Bezos thinks of new, innovative ways of making his employees work even harder. And if sales drop incrementally, he lays people off. But I'll defer talking about his trademark, sociopathic business model for another day.

Our focus is trying to get a handle on "big money". The challenge is: Exactly how do we put a mountain of cash into some frame of reference which allows us to process it, grasp it? How do we keep it from becoming a remote and inaccessible blur?

Let's leverage our earlier appreciation of a million dollars.

Elon Musk, as of this writing, is the richest man in the world and is worth an estimated $249,400,000,000. That's *$249.4 billion!* Okay . . . if we had full, unfettered access to all that money, and were to spend *$1 million a day*, every day without a break, how long would it take to go through Elon Musk's entire fortune?

Are you ready for this?

[Drum roll]

At $1 million a day, to spend $249.4 billion, it would take *683 years!*

The current life expectancy in the U.S. is 76.4 years. Making the obviously impossible assumption that a person would start spending $1 million a day from the day he or she exited the womb, and keep up the pace over the entire course of their life, right up to their last gasp and final heart palpitation, it would take *almost 9 lifetimes* to spend Elon Musk's money.

Did that help?

Probably not. 9 lifetimes? Almost 7 centuries?

We're still stuck in the Twilight Zone.

Let's shift gears. How about this?

If we stacked $1 bills, $1 million would be almost 25 feet high.

$1 billion would be over 4½ miles high, up where jetliners fly.

Does any of this help us get some perspective?

You probably wonder ... what is the point of these exercises? It's this ...

On subsequent pages, we're going to be constantly talking about millions, billions, trillions of dollars.

As we pointed out in the previous chapter, when we engage with numbers of this scale, they tend to become a blur, an abstraction. Just big numbers.

A million here. A billion there. What's a few trillion between friends?

We can't let that happen.

When we start looking at the enormity of our governmental budgets, when we get into the cost of our defense, the appalling price tags on our wars, the zeroes will pile up and our heads will begin to spin.

We must somehow fight this, maintain focus, fully grasp the magnitude of the crisis, the scale of the problem, the monstrousness of the irresponsibility and abuse of power, and the social and personal devastation that is unfolding around us as a result.

Because, if we lose perspective now, we're going to lose our country.

Every person is precious. Every life is precious. Yet we live in a society where there's a price tag on everything, even basic rights, even basic survival. Every dollar that could go toward sustaining and nurturing us – each of us equally special and invaluable – is likewise precious and invaluable. It's time to stop squandering our vast resources and wealth, stop mortgaging our future, and stop consigning our great experiment in democratic self-government to the dustbin of history.

Brown University's Cost of War Project

The Costs of War Project at Brown University's Watson Institute[1] is one of the most valuable research endeavors in modern times. We will be referencing their incredibly lucid and well-documented analysis throughout this book.

This is from the front page of their website …

Some of the Costs of War Project's main findings include:

- At least 929,000 people have died due to direct war violence, including armed forces on all sides of the conflicts, contractors, civilians, journalists, and humanitarian workers.
- Many times more have died indirectly in these wars, due to ripple effects like malnutrition, damaged infrastructure, and environmental degradation.
- Over 387,000 civilians have been killed in direct violence by all parties to these conflicts.
- Over 7,050 U.S. soldiers have died in the wars.
- We do not know the full extent of how many U.S. service members returning from these wars became injured or ill while deployed.
- Many deaths and injuries among U.S. contractors have not been reported as required by law, but it is likely that approximately 8,000 have been killed.
- 38 million people have been displaced by the post-9/11 wars in Afghanistan, Pakistan, Iraq, Syria, Libya, Yemen, Somalia and the Philippines.
- The U.S. government is conducting counterterror activities in 85 countries, vastly expanding this war across the globe.
- The post-9/11 wars have contributed significantly to climate change. The Defense Department is one of the world's top greenhouse gas emitters.
- The wars have been accompanied by erosions in civil liberties and human rights at home and abroad.
- The human and economic costs of these wars will continue for decades with some costs, such as the financial costs of U.S. veterans' care, not peaking until mid-century.
- Most U.S. government funding of reconstruction efforts in Iraq and Afghanistan has gone towards arming security forces in both countries. Much of the money allocated to humanitarian relief and rebuilding civil society has been lost to fraud, waste, and abuse.
- The cost of the post-9/11 wars in Iraq, Afghanistan, Pakistan, Syria, and elsewhere totals about $8 trillion. This does not include future interest costs on borrowing for the wars.
- The ripple effects on the U.S. economy have also been significant, including job loss and interest rate increases.
- U.S. policymakers scarcely considered alternatives to war in the aftermath of 9/11 or in debating the invasion of Iraq. Some of those alternative paradigms for addressing the problem of terror attacks are still available to the U.S.

Impressive, eh?

Their studies look at all of the consequences of military aggression, the death and destruction *directly* inflicted on people, the death and suffering *indirectly* resulting from wars, the vast numbers forced from their homes and homelands fleeing the conflict zones, the economic and infrastructural devastation that occurs in a nation under attack, and since these days the U.S. seems to have its fingers in just about every military confrontation going on around the world, the huge financial burden inflicted by war and excess militarization on us as a nation. As we will see, the numbers are staggering.

The focus of this book is almost exclusively the last of these, i.e. the financial burden borne by U.S. citizens, resulting from our out-of-control military. There are three reasons for this.

First, what happens "here", meaning at home in the lives of everyday people, is vastly more important to the majority of citizens than what happens "over there", in some remote country or some far-away battlefield. Before I take this further, let me be absolutely clear: I'm not judging anyone. Every person has their own view of life, their own agenda, their own values and world view. Real people living real lives in real time have challenges and crises which of necessity demand their immediate focus and are their first priority. As I say on the Peace Dividend website,[2] "People can't feel much empathy for cholera victims in Yemen or refugees in Syria, when members of their own immediate family are suffering. Everyday folks can't pay attention to our aggressions in the South China Sea and Russia's borders, when they need to pay attention to keeping a job and food on the table." Moreover, while spending on military conflicts "over there" may not seem to have an immediate impact on citizens here in America, or be noticed at all, lacking the money they need to survive right here at home can't be missed. The bills come due, the kids need new shoes, the car breaks down. A member of the family requires expensive medical attention. There's not enough money to cover it all. Pull out the credit cards. Then the credit card payments come due. It's a never-ending struggle just to make ends meet.

In terms of the federal budget, most people don't have the time, energy or interest to sit down and analyze the Omnibus Spending Bill[3] or the NDAA (National Defense Authorization Act).[4] Moreover, by constantly peddling a highly distracting and deceptive narrative, the establishment makes sure that the real costs of our war machine and world-conquering imperial agenda – and how this is a colossal drain on our whole society and everyone in it – are hidden behind patriotic mumbo-jumbo and jingoistic cheerleading. Everyday folks certainly sense things aren't right but don't have enough information to accurately assess the true causes and assign blame for the mess – though we'll show the truth of the matter is hiding in plain sight. *War is making them poor! War is making all of us poor!*

Secondly, a major reason people are not outraged by how much war and militarism directly hurts them, their families, their schools and communities, is that most people have NO IDEA how much the U.S. actually spends on defense, preparation for war, and fabricating the conditions for conflict and military confrontation in the world. It's the fog of "big numbers" and the smokescreen of propaganda. Yet the evidence of waste and calculated deception is abundant and inescapably incriminating. We'll lay it out big and bold so there's no doubt or ambiguity, and the public can be as appalled and angry as I am.

The third reason for "following the money" is that the fraud of war, the military excess, and grotesque waste within the DOD, and the calculated lying which has gone into propping up this house of marked cards, provide all the justification "we the people" need to clean house – to give these con artists and sociopathic empire builders their walking papers. True, there is a wide range of malfeasance in many areas of our current governance. But most other abuses of power are more nuanced, usually a great deal more convoluted and technical. We can only properly investigate and address the other widespread misconduct when we have elected officials who *work for us*, not the rich and powerful – representatives who have the courage and integrity to tell it like it is, then put things right, *across the board* in all areas of government.

On the other hand, the wrecking ball the DOD/MIC and imperial project have taken to the American Dream is so easy to grasp, so obvious, so catastrophic, so shameful, once the facts are known and citizens are united for action, my hope is that the crooks and liars promoting the military madness will all be thrown out on their heels. Then it will be up to us regular folks to install a true "people's government", one that works for you and me, not the big banks, not Wall Street, not the military-industrial complex. This will be a people's government which rejects the war economy, which doesn't see the solution to every problem as buying more unneeded military junk, building more military bases, dropping more bombs on other countries, and acting as the policeman for the world. This will be the beginning of a new era of deep and dramatic reform, a long overdue renewal of our unique experiment in self-government, a reinventing of our country. It will be a massive effort which will likely stretch out for decades.

So ... the three reasons for focusing on how 'war is making us poor' are:

1) 200,000,000 or more everyday citizens will pay attention.
2) The amount of money involved is massive and game changing.
3) Targeting this abuse of trust is how the people regain power.

More Bases More Bombs More War

The current trajectory of U.S. military and foreign policy is obvious.

Driven purely by institutional self-preservation, the relentless pursuit of profits by the military-industrial-complex, and an obsession with being the imperial overlord of the entire world, the cancer of American military presence continues to metastasize[1] unchecked across the planet. Not satisfied with creating tens of thousands of new terrorists since 9/11 with aggressive wars, invasions, special ops initiatives, drone bombing, assassinations – all claiming the lives of over a million innocent civilians – budgetary allocations are in place and plans being implemented for even more bases in Asia, Africa, Europe, even the Arctic.

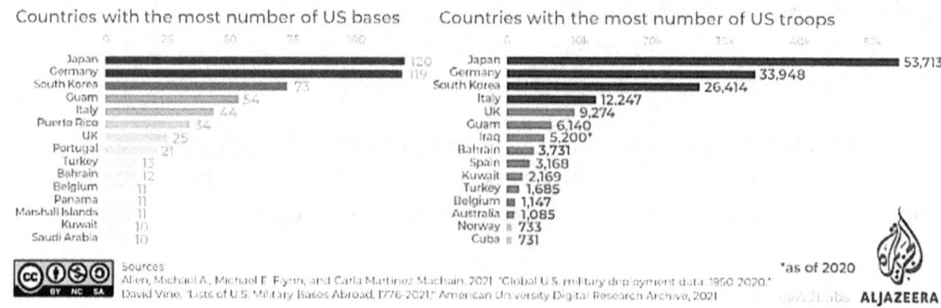

Is it any surprise that when America sets up a new military hub in a foreign country, conflict and war soon follow?

It's a closed feedback loop where a cure sets up the conditions for the disease it's supposed to treat. If an area is relatively at peace, the putative guarantees of continuing tranquility offered by a military presence will produce opposition and rivalry which inevitably will metastasize into conflict and war.

On that note, there certainly is no mystery why terrorism is on the rise, especially in Middle Eastern countries.

Osama bin Laden stated it clearly. So have Syria, Iraq, Afghanistan, China, Russia, and many countries in our own hemisphere.

To paraphrase: "We don't want you here."

Not only is sovereignty at issue in these native lands, but often they host sites which are considered sacred in both social and political traditions which stretch back centuries. The very presence of U.S. soldiers, war planes, drones, or any of the other paraphernalia of empire is insult enough. But the slaughter of innocent individuals, too often women and children, can only evoke cries of outrage and demands for revenge. Is it asking too much to imagine how U.S. citizens would react if a wedding party was blown to bits[2] in Topeka, Kansas or Knoxville, Tennessee?

This must end. The unnecessary expansion of U.S. military presence throughout the world is bankrupting our economy, incriminating each and every American citizen in horrifying war crimes, risking World War III, and ultimately will collapse the nation and take down the great American experiment.

Let's now look at the impact domestically of the hyper-militarization, expansion of U.S. imperial reach, seemingly limitless increase in military expenditures, and endless wars.

Federal Debt

How does the richest, most powerful nation in history end up saddling itself with more than \$34 trillion in federal government debt?[1] Why does the U.S. have to borrow money if it's so wealthy? What are the consequences short and long term for such a debt burden?

The current economic system – and I include the entire global framework which is integrated de facto and by default into a massive, internally and externally self-reinforcing, pan-dependent, co-dependent, extremely robust, arguably indestructible edifice – did not arrive as a package. It was not some planned, conceptualized, prototyped, rigorously tested, methodically improved mechanism built around pre-conceived goals and rational expectations. The "economy" is more of a Frankenstein's monster or Rube Goldberg Machine.[2]

Like most complex human inventions, it developed by gradual degrees in tiny increments, pieced together bit by bit over millennia, a summing of human interactions and transactions, driving and driven by behaviors, customs, protocols, agreements, mechanisms, formal and informal rules, institutions, and eventually the body of law which buttresses the entire mercantile system with the agency of judicial enforcement. The current economic model is not rational or irrational, because it was not premised on logic or rationality. Its multipolar parentage is rooted in whim, convenience, necessity, habit, pragmatism, common sense, uncommon avarice and psychopathy, respect, ruthlessness, morality, amorality, trust, distrust, altruism, self-interest, malevolence, and just about every other manifestation of *homo sapiens'* capacity to act.

Criticizing the dominant economic model is child's play. Replacing it is virtually impossible. People who should know better offer comments like: 'What about Marx?' or 'Doesn't MMT make more sense?' or 'Socialism will get us where we want to be!' or 'There are much better ways to go about this.'

Easily said. But saying is not doing. And what we have, what is wreaking havoc with the environment, what is preventing many longstanding challenges and crimes against humanity from being addressed – war, famine, preventable diseases, grotesque wealth inequality – what is for better or worse churning away to the tune of over \$100 trillion a year worldwide, is benefitting _someone_. It's making and keeping _some folks_ very, very rich! We even know who they are. We know that their numbers are relatively small, but that they reap incomprehensibly huge rewards from the current system. This one statistic – referencing the U.S. economy – captures the skewed reality of the current arrangement perfectly: The richest three individuals in the U.S. have more personal wealth than the 160,000,000 in the bottom half of the economy.[3]

We also know and must keep *first and foremost in mind* that those who are beneficiaries of the current economic system, those who are piling up vast and accelerating fortunes from the oppression and misery of others, those who – to cite the component which is our focus here – make colossal profits from war and immersing the world in chaos, death and destruction. And these people HAVE THE POWER! At the very least, they have sufficient power to fend off any real challenges to their supremacy and thus maintain a status quo that is massively favorable to them. They control enough of government, media, the military, the police, etc. to keep the war gravy trains running a full schedule and on time.

Let me be clear. I can't for one second accept what is going on with the economies of both the world and more specifically the U.S. as the "best we can possibly do" or even "the best we can do for now". Anything promoting this fiction is a calculated and colossal lie.

But it's not going to change just because there's a better idea, or a more rational approach, or a more humane way to conduct our affairs.

It's only going to change when those who are generously rewarded by the way that system is now configured, those who wield their wealth and power to keep the system working for them, are no longer able to exercise their power. It will only change when *the current ruling class are stripped of their hammerlock grip on the system*, and replaced with individuals who reflect the values and priorities of the rest of us. It is only going to change when "we the people" figure out how to uproot the existing tyranny by the rich and powerful – despite the existing, admittedly onerous limitations on our ability to protest, challenge, and generate deep, decisive democratic reform.

Thus, as we move this discussion forward, starting with the appalling and absurd handling of our economic affairs at the national level, our activist responses must of necessity be tempered by current realities. We operate within these boundaries because we have no choice. The system is not going to change itself, and our appeals to those in power to do the right thing fall on deaf ears. Appealing to the common decency of the ruling elite is a waste of energy. They have none. Our only way forward is to slog through the obstacles and identify fatal vulnerabilities in the system, then decide the best ways to use them to our advantage.

One caveat: the system could be overturned via a revolution. Because of the complexity of our society, the existing concentration of power, the availability of tools introduced by new technologies, and the ruthless determination of those now in control, it would be a revolution of unprecedented violence, bloodier and more destructive than any in human history. I recognize that it is very possible – some believe inevitable – things could eventually come to this. For now, we should rigorously and zealously explore every other possible option, to avoid the horrendous carnage which would result from a violent insurrection.

Let's get started.

• • •

Despite only having 5% of the world's population, the U.S. is responsible for 25.4% of the world's economy.[4] The ubiquity of American corporate power equates to incalculable influence and economic control across the globe.

So here is a reasonable question …

How is it possible owning such a major chunk of the global economy – currently the U.S. comes in at $26.85 trillion annually and that of the whole world $105.569 trillion – the U.S. government couldn't at least break even?

The simple answer is that less money came in than went out. This is manifestly true but trivializes the irresponsibility and recklessness of the decisions which led to the catastrophic mess we find ourselves in.

What set the stage over many decades for our current calamity is a complex, often self-contradictory, ultimately self-destructive web of good intentions, bad intentions, self-serving agendas, sinister manipulations, rationalizations, loopy fantasies, skewed incentives, foolishness, innocence and cunning, married to callous and calculated deception of the general public by those who reap the rewards of the current arrangement. Most of the narratives about the wonders of neoliberalism capitalism and the economic miracle supposedly underway are fairy tales for mass consumption by the gullible and uniformed masses.

The impact of this massive deception – I bluntly refer to it as a con – on the population is a level of poverty that is shocking. The U.S. incessantly trumpets itself as the richest nation in history. Let's look at the reality.

In *Poverty, By America*,[5] Princeton University social scientist and urban ethnographer Matt Desmond writes: "If America's poor founded a country, that country would have a bigger population than Australia or Venezuela. Almost one in nine Americans – including one in eight children – live in poverty. There are more than 38 million people living in the United States who cannot afford basic necessities, and more than 108 million getting by on $55,000 a year or less, many stuck in that space between poverty and security. More than a million of our public schoolchildren are homeless, living in motels, cars, shelters, and abandoned buildings."

Yes, a truly honest portrait of our country is appalling: America is broke, countless citizens are struggling, millions are close to or living in poverty.

If the U.S. has so much wealth, where is it? Where has the money gone? Where is the money going?

The details of this travesty and tragedy would fill volumes. But we only have to look at one broad aspect of it, because it represents the largest single component of the squandering and theft of our national resources. Moreover, those directly responsible for it are the same ones culpable for the entire mess.

In a twisted way, this is good news. It means we can identify the enemy. Once they are taken out of the equation – ostracism? exile? imprisonment? – we can initiate a sober, rational, balanced, impartial look at our economy and decide democratically what it should look like and how it should function, with an eye to creating a social and economic environment that serves *all* of the people of our nation, not just a privileged few.

Let's now look at that "one broad aspect" of our economic dystopia.

•••

From the Brown University Costs of War Project[6]: "Through Fiscal Year 2022, the United States federal government has spent and obligated $8 trillion dollars on the post-9/11 wars in Afghanistan, Pakistan, Iraq and elsewhere. This figure includes: direct Congressional war appropriations; war-related increases to the Pentagon base budget; veterans care and disability; increases in the homeland security budget; interest payments on direct war borrowing; foreign assistance spending; and estimated future obligations for veterans' care."

$8 TRILLION DOLLARS!

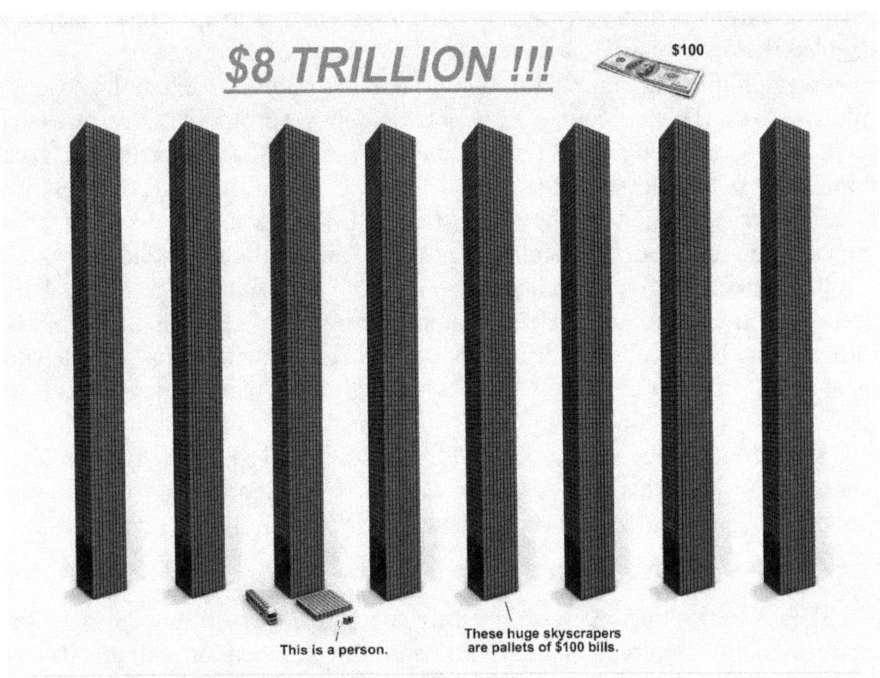

Let's take stock.

<u>AFGHANISTAN</u>: After 20 years of occupation and relatively low-level conflict – which left 243,000 Afghanis (and Pakistanis)[7] and 2,448 U.S. soldiers dead[8] – we left Afghanistan in shame. We accomplished nothing. Begging the question: Why were we there in the first place? The story kept changing. First it was to capture the monster, Osama bin Laden. The Taliban offered to turn him over to the U.S.[9] but that was too easy. We went ahead anyway and invaded. Then at some point we decided we were there to establish democracy. Out of this emerged talk about women's rights and making it possible for girls to go to school. Or stroll around without having to wear a hijab or burka.[10] As if the U.S. should decide which religion practices and customs should be canceled and replaced in other countries. Go Team America!

<u>IRAQ</u>: The U.S. started its war on Iraq – the more recent one – with a shock-and-awe bombing campaign on March 19, 2003. We had to eliminate Saddam Hussein's non-existent weapons of mass destruction and punish him for 9/11 – though he had nothing to do with the attack on the Twin Towers – by removing him from power. Besides, he was so evil, he made Adolph Hitler look like a choir boy. Of course, not only were there no WMDs, Iraq had no way to deliver them to the American homeland, since FedEx had no offices there. When the WMDs ultimately proved to be impossible to find (like most things that don't exist), repeating our fiasco in Afghanistan we decided that in actuality we were there to liberate the Iraqi people – whether they wanted to be liberated or not – and remake Iraq as an exemplary model of democracy. This, of course, proved to be a fool's errand. Finally, however, there was acknowledgement that we didn't know why we were in Iraq. And though the war officially ended in 2011, the U.S. still has a troop presence there. This is justified by the need to fight ISIS, the most savage terrorist organization in modern history, a political and military leviathan which resulted directly from the chaos and power vacuum the U.S. created by destroying Iraq. With no sense of shame or irony, the U.S. military currently stationed in Iraq works with a host of terrorist organizations we used to oppose, in order to overthrow the Assad regime in neighboring Syria. An estimated 224,000-246,000 Iraqis died[11] from the war on Iraq, including as many as 204,575 civilians. 4,492 U.S. soldiers[12] lost their lives in this pointless military disaster. Somehow President George W. Bush once proudly declared: "Mission accomplished!" Good luck figuring out what that meant.

<u>SYRIA</u>: Speaking of Syria, operating out of Iraq and numerous bases established by illegally invading Syria itself, the U.S. continues to this day to "fight ISIS" – *(wink wink)* – squandering billions of dollars and slaughtering

thousands of Syrians along the way. Of course, thanks to Russia, Iran, and Syria, ISIS has been vanquished. So the real agenda of the U.S. is to weaken and topple Assad, then install a puppet regime which will do its bidding,[13] opening the gates for plunder by the usual predators. Currently, the U.S. militarily occupies 30% of Syria,[14] the most resource rich and agriculturally productive northeast region of the country. With typical ham-fisted candor, then-president Donald Trump admitted that the U.S. is there to steal Syria's oil.[15] Combining extremely harsh economic sanctions and depriving the Syrian people of the food stuffs grown in the occupied region, the U.S. continues to make every effort to starve Syria into submission,[16] so that its President Assad can be replaced with a U.S. puppet. Granted, when the "pro-democracy" protests began back in 2011, there were legitimate objections to the way the Assad regime was handling the country. This was an internal matter. But the U.S. has a way of making internal matters its own business, leveraging citizen discontent into regime change favorable on its own terms. The protests started peacefully. There is evidence that the crowds were "seeded" with external armed mercenaries,[17] which turned things violent. We see here our tax dollars at work, "spreading democracy" by fomenting insurrection. It never ends well. The streets end up littered with dead people, economies crash, patients die in hospitals, folks starve in their beds, the door is wide open for terrorist groups[18] like ISIS, Al-Qaeda, Jabhat al-Nusra, and other barbaric intruders – some of which the U.S. secretly supports.[19] The U.S. thinks such collateral damage and a few hardships are well worth the price,[20] so that democracy-starved foreigners can reap the rewards of embracing the American Way, whether they want to or not. As the indispensable nation,[21] we call the shots. The cruel reality is that the American taxpayer pays for all this chaos, human suffering and slaughter, to the tune of billions and billions of dollars.

• • •

We shouldn't for a moment think that such military misadventures – wars based on pure lies to serve twisted agendas – are anything unique in our history. A convincing case can be made that every instance of our military aggression since WWII – and there have been many – has been advanced by an artfully fabricated narrative and in many cases instigated by a false flag.

Two ignominious examples post-WWII deserve mention, since they are so starkly representative of ideology-driven U.S. madness and paranoia.

CHINA, 1945-46	PERU, 1965	BOSNIA, 1995
SYRIA, 1949	GREECE, 1967	IRAQ, 1998
KOREA, 1950-53	GUATEMALA, 1967-69	SUDAN, 1998
CHINA, 1950-53	CAMBODIA, 1969-70	AFGHANISTAN, 1998
IRAN, 1953	CHILE, 1970-73	YUGOSLAVIA, 1999
GUATEMALA, 1954	ARGENTINA, 1976	AFGHANISTAN, 2001
TIBET, 1955-70s	ANGOLA, 1976-92	IRAQ, 2002-03
INDONESIA, 1958	TURKEY, 1980	YEMEN, 2002-20
CUBA, 1959	POLAND, 1980-81	HAITI, 2004
DEMOCRATIC	EL SALVADOR, 1981-92	SOMALIA, 2006-07
REPUBLIC OF	NICARAGUA, 1981-90	IRAN, 2005-PRESENT
CONGO, 1960-65	CAMBODIA, 1980-95	HONDURAS, 2009
DOMINICAN	LEBANON, 1982-84	LIBYA, 2011
REPUBLIC, 1961	GRENADA, 1983-84	SYRIA, 2011-PRESENT
VIETNAM, 1961-73	LIBYA, 1986	BRAZIL, 2016
BRAZIL, 1964	IRAN, 1987-88	BOLIVIA, 2019
BRITISH GUIANA, 1964	LIBYA, 1989	VENEZUELA, 2019
REPUBLIC OF	PHILIPPINES, 1989	GUYANA, 2020
CONGO, 1964	PANAMA, 1989-90	IRAQ, 2020
GUATEMALA, 1964	HAITI, 1991	SOMALIA, 2020
LAOS, 1964-73	IRAQ, 1991	AFGHANISTAN, 2020
DOMINICAN	KUWAIT, 1991	
REPUBLIC, 1965-66	SOMALIA, 1992-94	
INDONESIA, 1965	IRAQ, 1992-96	

<u>KOREAN WAR</u>: The Korean War[22] (1950-1953) extinguished the lives of an estimated 1.5 million North Koreans, 1.2 million South Koreans, 600,000 Chinese and 36,574 U.S. combat troops.[23] The U.S. spent $389 billion dollars[24] for the war effort. While it's true that North Korea attacked South Korea in order to take control of and unite the two Koreas, one extremely vital element is always missing from the official U.S. narrative.[25] North Korea was betrayed by America. Many citizens of both North and South Korea wanted unification of the peninsula. However, a nationwide election, including both North and South wasn't permitted by the U.S., which feared based on polls, that it would favor the Communist leadership. The U.S. preferred to keep their corrupt US-puppet in power in Seoul. This mortal phobia and hatred of the commies represented the initial manifestation of the Domino Theory, the hysteria-level fear that if one country turned to Communism, then like dominoes falling one-after-the-other, countless countries would join in and create a tsunami of the dread red ideology. While there is dispute about who fired the first shot,[26] North Korea did invade in force, backed by China and Russia, then the U.S. stepped up to the plate and unleashed an air war that demolished everything taller than a kimchi stand, including dams and other vital infrastructural assets, and even threw in both biological and chemical weapons for good measure.[27] America stopped short of nuking the piles of rubble and corpses they had created, but only barely. General Douglas MacArthur, wanted to bomb his way from Korea into China, by dropping 30 to 50 tactical nuclear bombs.[28] President Truman nixed both the idea and MacArthur, relieving him as Unified Theater Commander.

Even without the nuking, least 1.5 million innocent civilians died from the aerial blitz, bioweapons, and starvation. Like so many of our wars to make the rest of the world safe for "democracy", things didn't go quite as planned. North Korea is still communist. But no dominoes fell. Tragically the prospects for total war breaking out again on the peninsula is still a constant threat – the U.S. has for seven decades refused to negotiate a final peace treaty[29] to put an end to the tensions – and North Korea has been forced to develop more advanced weapons to defend itself, including even usable nuclear bombs and long-range missiles to deliver them. The final slap in the face is that the rest of the world is beginning to clearly see the U.S. for what it is: a bellicose, belligerent, bullying aggressor. It's our way or bombs away!

<u>VIETNAM</u>: Until the Iraq War of 2003, the Vietnam War[30] ranked as likely the biggest foreign policy blunder in our history. It was an embarrassment, a debacle, a tragedy – a complete waste of over $840 billion.[31] Upwards of 3.3 million Vietnamese were killed, countless more were mutilated and maimed. Tens of thousands of Vietnamese still suffer

birth defects from America's prolific use of Agent Orange, a highly toxic herbicide/defoliant. Thousands of U.S. combat troops were also poisoned by it. They were the lucky ones. 57,979 servicemen died in this pointless war. Driven again by irrational fear of the spread of communism, it was a war of choice – a horrible choice – the lessons of which apparently have been forgotten.

President John F. Kennedy intended to pull all U.S. troops out of Vietnam, as part of a comprehensive rehabilitation of U.S. policy, a whole new direction which would inaugurate peaceful co-existence with our enemies, reduction of nuclear arsenals, and meaningful steps toward disarmament. This hopeful vision of a world living in harmony was introduced and summed up in his extraordinary commencement speech at American University,[32] June 1963.

> *"I am talking about genuine peace, the kind of peace that makes life on earth worth living, the kind that enables men and nations to grow and to hope and build a better life for their children — not merely peace for Americans but peace for all men and women — not merely peace in our time but peace for all time."*

Having survived in the first half of his presidency the Bay of Pigs fiasco,[33] then the near brush with nuclear annihilation augured by the Cuban Missile Crisis,[34] Kennedy realized that the prevailing policies were a prescription for just more mistrust, confrontation, conflict, and potential Armageddon. Time to reverse course and entirely change the trajectory of the country. The pursuit of peace[35] would define the remainder of his time in office. The warmongers could see the writing on the wall. Kennedy was soon assassinated and denied the opportunity to bring his vision of a peaceful world to fruition. The consequences were dire. The war in Vietnam ramped up and would consume vast amounts of money, time, and human life, then eventually end up in a colossal, humiliating defeat. Confidence in the U.S. as a world power was dealt a major blow, both at home and across the globe. More dark irony: While all of Vietnam – not just the north – now embraced communism, again the dominoes didn't exactly tumble. China had been communist[36] since 1949. Laos embraced communism[37] in 1975. That was it. The official reason for needing to intervene in Vietnam proved to be spurious. I lived in Vietnam for six months and have visited several other times. It's rather much like any other country, certainly not a fearsome, oppressive regime of tyranny and terror. The party that is most obvious is not the Communist Party, but the ones going on in the night clubs, street bazaars, shopping malls, and the Bui Vien backpacker area in Ho Chi Minh City (Saigon).

· · ·

Back to the present.

Afghanistan. Iraq. Libya. Syria. Yemen. Somalia. Ukraine.

Here's the stark, undeniable reality …
NONE OF THESE WARS AND CONFLICTS HAD TO BE FOUGHT.
Period!
None of these countries or their leaders posed a threat to the American homeland. None of them attacked – would *dare* to attack – the United States. Even on the international stage, none of them were particularly hostile or critical of the U.S., except when America was seen as meddling in their internal affairs.

All of these were wars, confrontations, and military interventions *of choice*.

We had our reasons. We initiated the crises. We decided something "had to be done". We decided that to get our way meant sending in the cruise missiles, fighter jets, drones, bombs, then the troops. We only play the diplomatic card to pave the way for war or to garner favorable public opinion, both at home and internationally. We don't have time or patience for negotiation, compromise, cooperation. We talk to other countries down the barrel of a gun.

Afghanistan. Iraq. Libya. Syria. Yemen. Somalia. Ukraine.

To rub salt in our wounds, nothing resembling a success or a victory can be claimed on any of these battlefields. That includes Ukraine. Because by the time this book is published, in all likelihood Ukraine as a functioning nation will no longer exist. Russia will have crushed the Ukrainian military, even though it was trained, backed, equipped, and funded by the US and its NATO lackeys.[38]

What are we to make of America's dismal, embarrassing, abject failure at the only thing it seems capable of doing? When is the payday for the U.S. addiction to war, and our apparent allergy to treating other countries with basic respect, our disregard for international law, our inability to honor treaties and commitments? Is there some "hidden glory", some redeeming facet to all of this war war war – *endless war!* – that I've somehow managed to miss?

Our international reputation is in freefall.

Our belief in ourselves as a force for good is increasingly shaky.

Our confidence in our military might is an exercise in self-delusion.

Exactly what good has come of all our bullying, bombing, and bombast?

Unless you call since 9/11 turning 38 million people into refugees,[39] the slaughter of over 905,000 people,[40] mostly innocent civilians, unless you consider spending $8 trillion[41] … on … on … what? … an achievement of some sorts, we have nothing to show but disgrace and our nation's steady descent into insolvency.

Yes, war and wanton aggression are bankrupting America at every level.

The focus of this book is on the economic impact of such folly and fraud.

Because while the bankrupting of America in other respects tends to be less tangible, there is nothing abstract about poverty, hunger, want, homelessness, broken spirits and hopelessness – the inability to achieve a decent life and fulfill our potential as citizens of the allegedly wealthiest nation in history. Our appalling powerlessness and massive failure are the direct result of economic deprivation and impoverishment, much of which can be traced squarely to endless war and monomaniacal pursuit of Pax Americana empire.

State and Municipal Government Debt

The introduction of the Truth in Accounting[1] *Financial State of the States 2020* – the 11th annual attempt by this organization to bring some realistic and credible perspective on the solvency of state governments – offers this summary:

> "At the end of the fiscal year (FY) 2019, 39 states did not have enough money to pay all of their bills. This means that to balance the budget — as is required by law in 49 states — elected officials have not included the true costs of the government in their budget calculations and have pushed costs onto future taxpayers."

Mind you, they were looking at fiscal year 2019 – *before the Covid-19 crisis!* The response to the virus over the next three years just made the outlook much much worse.

The condition of cities across America was equally abysmal. This is from the 6th annual report of Truth in Accounting *Financial State of the Cities 2022:*

> "Cities, in general, did not have enough money to pay all of their bills. Based on our latest analysis, the total debt among the 75 most populous cities amounted to $357 billion. (Our analysis does not include capital assets or related debt.) Most of this debt comes from unfunded retirement benefit promises, such as pension and retiree healthcare debt. For FY 2020, pension debt accounted for $194.9 billion, and other post-employment benefits (OPEB) totaled $164.8 billion."

Meaning, for fiscal year 2020 – June 1, 2019 to June 30, 2020 – 61 out of the 75 most populous cities in the U.S. were underwater. Again, this report mostly reflected conditions before the devastating impact of Covid-19 on the economies of cities, states, and the federal government. While $357 billion of debt doesn't compare to the $34 trillion in federal government debt – at least in absolute numbers – it still represents poor judgement, poor management, a tax-wary public, and a level of dysfunction that is an insult to the everyday citizen.

• • •

Should we be surprised by the fix these state governments are in? Hardly!

It's the same old story. Governments at all levels overspend for a host of reasons. Politicians across the spectrum try to appease the citizenry by keeping taxes low. When spending outpaces income, shortfalls are inevitable.

What are state and municipal governments to do when addressing the discrepancy? No surprise here in the least. *They borrow the money.* At interest, of course!

They "kick the can down the road", as the expression goes. Which is a clever euphemism meaning they have "have pushed costs onto future taxpayers." But not just the burden of the initial shortfall. Future taxpayers will have to bear the costs of "debt service", the interest on whatever borrowing instrument is engaged – usually it's a bond.

How big of a problem is this? It takes little imagination or accounting skill to recognize that with the states and cities, as with the federal government, debt just piles up more debt. Services which are fundamental to a functioning society will just become less affordable as time goes on, perhaps disappear entirely.

Now here's an important question: How does this impact the functioning of our nation and the welfare of its citizens at a local level?

Let's take a quick but honest look at the condition of the U.S. in these tumultuous, contentious times. Just a few of the important indicators . . .

<u>POVERTY</u>: In 2022 child poverty in America hit a historic low. This was directly due to massive intervention by governments at all levels to mitigate the economic devastation wrought by the response to the Covid-19 pandemic. But all those programs were allowed to lapse. The overall poverty rate and the child poverty rate shot up and both now stand at 12.4%.[2] This means one out of eight U.S. citizens live at or below the official poverty line, an artificial threshold which many believe is an unrealistically low one at that.

Poverty varies considerably from state to state. But California, which is often regarded as the economically most robust of the 50 states, now leads the nation. One out of every five Californians – 20.6% – live in poverty.[3] As the most populous state,[4] this means over 8 million folks in California are poor.

Florida comes in second at 19%, with Louisiana and New York tied for third at 17.9%. In Washington DC – not a state but embarrassingly our nation's capital – 22.2% are reported to be living in impoverished conditions.

Tragically, this translates to a lot of children going to bed hungry every night.

Food shortage disproportionately affects black and Latino kids. The USDA reported that in 2022, 29% of Black children and similarly 26% of Latino children were food insecure.

Then there's a phenomenon which America has not witnessed since the Great Depression. According to a Harris Poll conducted for Bloomberg News,[5] roughly 45% of young people ages 18 - 29 are living at home with their parents. The reasons, as CBS News reports it[6]: "The top reason for returning home, at more than 40%, is to save money, Harris found. In addition, 30% of respondents said they are staying with family members because they can't afford to live on their own. Other factors included paying down debt (19%), recovering financially from emergency costs (16%) and losing a job (10%), according to the survey."

What happened to the American Dream? The Land of Opportunity?

<u>HEALTH AND NUTRITION</u>: Americans simply are not very healthy. This despite spending more as a percentage of GDP[7] – 16.9% – on health care than any other peer country. Switzerland at 12.2% runs a distant second. On average Americans spend $9,523 per person a year[8] on medical expenses.

Specifically, poor health in the U.S. is the result of these factors: adverse birth outcomes, injuries and homicides, adolescent pregnancy and sexually transmitted infections, drug-related mortality, obesity and diabetes, heart disease, chronic lung disease, disabilities such as arthritis and other activity limiting debilities, high rates of HIV/AIDS infection.

A 2013 panel report by the National Academy of Sciences[9] compares health statistics in 16 high-income democracies in western Europe, as well as Australia, Canada and Japan. In many cases, the U.S. ranks last. Per Dr. Steven H. Woolf, chair of the committee that wrote the report: "The U.S. is doing worse than these other countries both in terms of life expectancy and health throughout their entire lives. This is a pervasive problem from birth to old age; it affects everyone and has been a long-standing problem." Globally, America ranks #35 in terms of overall citizen health.[10]

There's no excuse for this. Dr. Woolf again: "The fact is, people are dying earlier than they should be and suffering at rates that are avoidable. They are suffering from diseases we know how to prevent and then dying unnecessarily."

For example, on average the adult obesity rate in America is 42.4%. From the CDC[11]: "Obesity-related conditions include heart disease, stroke, type 2 diabetes and certain types of cancer. These are among the leading causes of preventable, premature death."

So … what's missing from the equation? Universal health care, equality of access regardless of income, healthier diets that include fresh ingredients and far less processed and pre-packaged foods, strict regulations limiting the use of prescription drugs, and most of all awareness, meaning awareness of good nutrition, the importance of regular exercise, awareness of the deleterious effects of anxiety, stress, depression, and common lifestyle choices.

Also sorely lacking is respect by the U.S. – at all levels of government – for Article 25 of the United Nations Universal Declaration of Human Rights[12]:

> Everyone has the right to a standard of living adequate for the health and well-being of himself and of his family, including food, clothing, housing and medical care and necessary social services, and the right to security in the event of unemployment, sickness, disability, widowhood, old age, or other lack of livelihood in circumstances beyond his control.

LONGEVITY: Directly related to the poor health and nutrition of America's population is how long – or how short – their stay is on this planet.

Longevity – how long people on average live – is declining in America. This contrasts with every other developed country in the world. The U.S. ranks 47th in the world,[13] with the average lifespan of males now standing at 77.27, females 82.23 years. By comparison, in Hong Kong, which is #1, males live on average to be 83.00 and females 88.66. In Japan, which is #3 in the world and where I permanently reside, males live to be 81.91 and females 87.97 years of age. Practically everywhere except in America longevity is steadily increasing.

Preventable diseases, understandably, account for the bulk of early deaths. These include heart disease, cancer, accidents, stroke, chronic lower respiratory diseases, Alzheimer's, diabetes, liver disease and cirrhosis, kidney disease.

But there are other factors.

Here's a shocker: More than 250,000 deaths in the U.S. every year are caused by medical error. That makes it the third leading cause of death.[14]

And suicide is on the rise. Since 2000, it has increased 38.6%, resulting in 49,449 deaths in 2022.[15] In 2021, there were an estimated 1.7 million suicide attempts. Suicide has recently dramatically increased among young people.[16] Nothing like young folks killing themselves to drag the longevity figures into the basement.

Here's another tragic statistic: In 2022, 109,680 died of drug overdoses.[17] Deaths from drug abuse has steadily increased every year since the 1970s (except for 2018). Currently fentanyl, a synthetic opioid is the main culprit.[18] Drug users 25-44 years of age account for most of the deaths.[19]

People would live longer if they were healthier in mind and body, and had a proper understanding of their physiology and the importance of what goes into and shouldn't go into their bodies. Knowledge is power and is one of the main drivers of human agency. There is a word for increasing such knowledge and understanding. It is …

EDUCATION: Public schools are being closed across the U.S. because of a lack of funds.

In 2013 with a shortfall of $1.4 billion, Philadelphia closed 23 schools.[20]

That same year, Chicago closed 49 elementary schools.

Since 2000, Detroit has closed almost 200 public schools.[21] The closures were inevitable with the exodus of manufacturing jobs, the dramatic shrinking of the tax base, the city facing decline and decay, despite neighborhood efforts at recovery and rejuvenation.

Responding to the Covid-19 crisis,[22] 44 states, the District of Columbia, Guam, Puerto Rico, Northern Marianas, and other U.S. territories, initiated blanket school closures in 2019/2020. Some of those schools never reopened.

This is just a sampling of the ongoing crisis in public education[23] unfolding across the U.S. at this time. As of 2021-22, 755 schools have been permanently shuttered.[24] At this point, it looks like more of the same coming.

As philosopher and educator John Dewey said …

"Education is not preparation for life; education is life itself."

… which in a society where general education is taking a back seat to entertainment and commerce, and opportunities are the privilege of a tiny elite class, so many lives seem DOA and 'hope' just the hook in a sales pitch[25] of more of the same empty promises and dead-end dreams.

HIGHER EDUCATION: 24 countries provide free college education[26]: Austria, Argentina, Brazil, Czech Republic, Denmark, Luxembourg, Egypt, Kenya, Finland, France, Germany, Greece, Iceland, Malaysia, Morocco, Norway, Panama, Poland, Scotland, Slovenia, Spain, Sweden, Turkey, and Uruguay.

A truly revealing story with a tragic ending is Libya and its policy on higher education. Before 2011, the year when the US and NATO destroyed the country[27] and its socialist leader, Muammar Gaddafi, was murdered, all education in Libya was free, right up through university. If Libyans could not find the education they needed at home, the government funded them to go abroad – in total including living costs! Government largesse didn't stop there. Electricity was completely free. And under Gaddafi, whenever a Libyan bought a car, the government subsidized 50% of the price. Banks in Libya were state-owned and loans were given to all its citizens at *zero percent interest* by law. All health care was free. All newlyweds in Libya received the equivalent of $50,000 USD from the government to buy their first apartment, and to help start their family. Under Gaddafi, a mother who gave birth to a child received $5,000 USD. So, the wanton destruction of Libya says loud and clear what the US and its fellow neo-colonial predators think of a government who puts its citizens first.

Back to higher education. Let's look at America.

Instead of making higher education available to as many people as possible, the U.S. has a two-tiered system. There are the very best colleges, only affordable to the very wealthy. Then there are the rest, so expensive they are barely affordable to everyone else. Most students resort to taking out loans. Millions graduate and are saddled with huge debts[28] they will struggle to pay off over the next decade of their working life. Nearly 1 in 5 adults in the United States carry student loan debt. The average student loan debt is $28,950 and including both federal and private loans, the total comes to $1.75 trillion.[29]

Here's a thought: We all know that we can't use any of the nuclear weapons we have in our arsenal. Neither can our adversaries. No one can. If we even have a limited nuclear war, say an exchange of 150 to 200 nuclear bombs, it will result in a nuclear winter,[30] and human life will be next to impossible. Right now, the U.S. – to stay ahead of the "competition" – is spending $1.5 trillion to upgrade its already insanely lethal nuclear force.[31] This includes delivery systems and the nuclear bombs themselves. Let's take that money and forgive the better part of the $1.75 trillion in student loans for the debt they never should have had to incur in the first place.

HOMELESSNESS: Currently, the number of homeless people in America is staggering. Even so, it is not a problem which the federal government tries to deal with. Homelessness mostly negatively impacts cities and towns, which are then forced to use very limited resources to try to alleviate both the suffering of the homeless and the stresses foisted on the local communities themselves.

From a recent Department of Housing and Urban Development (HUD) report[32]: "On a single night in 2023, roughly 653,100 people – or about 20 of every 10,000 people in the United States – were experiencing homelessness."

For Blacks it's 48.24 per 10,000 and Native Americans 44.92 per 10,000. Most certainly with inflation and the other troubling problems with our economy, these numbers are expected to increase.

Geographical distribution is not even[33] by a long shot. Eleven states and the District of Columbia are higher than the 20 per 10,000 national average. DC tops the list, with California, Vermont, and Oregon close behind.[34]

In terms of cities,[35] Los Angeles and LA County currently boasts the most homeless, at last count 65,111. New York City is close behind at 61,840. However, the care afforded the homeless varies considerably. In New York City, only 5.4% live on the streets, the city providing some sort of sheltering. In Los Angeles and California overall, however, 67.3% are unsheltered,[36] accounting for the appalling number of tent cities there.

It is an understatement to say that homelessness in America amidst so much abundance and wealth is both scandalous and tragic. A very recent, extremely scathing United Nations report "admonishing the United States' record on a broad range of domestic and international issues"[37] related to human rights abuses and neglect, specifically cited the criminalization of

unhoused people, a common practice in most urban environments. To put a fine point on this disgrace, it is genuinely shocking to consider that with so many forlorn individuals who have no home, often through no fault of their own, there are over 16 million homes in America that are sitting unoccupied.[38]

Is there a solution to this grotesque negligence and insult to basic decency?

It has been estimated by HUD that homelessness could be eliminated for $20 billion annually.[39] Here's an idea: It currently costs $60 billion a year to operate and support America's fleet of 480 naval vessels.[40] How about if we mothball 160 of them and give everyone a place to live?

• • •

Can we blame all of America's crises and deficiencies on the military? Perhaps not directly.

But we certainly can blame our chronic *inability to find the money to fix things* on the endless wars and exorbitant DOD budgets.

All of the wars since WWII have been wars of choice – someone thought they were a good idea. With the collapse of the Soviet Union in 1992, we were presented with a historic opportunity. Without a major enemy, we could have reduced our military to just what was necessary to defend our borders. But the warmongers chose to grow the military, buy more superfluous military junk, build hundreds of bases around the world, and divide the entire world into military zones in preparation for world conquest.

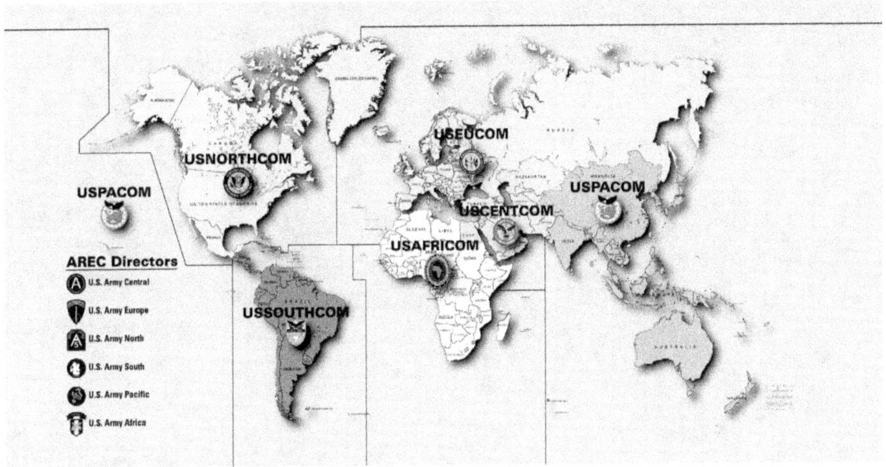

And what have we accomplished? Well, we didn't eradicate communism. Our military adventures have killed millions of people and displaced millions more as refugees. We destroyed whole cities and countries, spread chaos and division, and invited hatred for the U.S. across the globe. We've lost every war except our attack on the tiny island nation of Granada, if you can consider swooping in on a helpless nation with no defense force to speak of, a military victory. With the exception of our vassal NATO allies, the entire world either fears or despises us, usually both, viewing our one-sided, self-serving approach to international relations – "it's our way or bombs away" – as the arrogant behavior of a bellicose, bullying, would-be hegemon. We have totally squandered the good will and trust in the U.S., embraced by nearly everyone right after WWII and a couple of honeymoon decades that followed.

We've achieved all of this to the tune of trillions and trillions of dollars. Money which could have been spent on the America people, addressing the above mentioned and many other challenges which have been accruing and just becoming more pernicious and intractable.

Much of our $34+ trillion national debt – arguably the majority – is the direct result of unnecessary, illegal wars and pointless military expansion. Therefore, much of the $1+ trillion we now spend to service that debt is the direct result of unnecessary, illegal wars and pointless military expansion.

It's the same with state and municipal debt. We are throwing money to the wind while the needs of everyday citizens go unattended.

This has to stop! It is destroying our country. It is destroying our future!

WAR IS MAKING US POOR!

Whose Money Is It Anyway?

You've heard of 'the fog of war".

Let me introduce to you something I call 'the fog of government'.

This is the pervasive confusion about what our elected government officials are and what our relationship is with them.

When talking about government – though we supposedly embrace a democratic ideal, i.e. government by the governed – we often get pulled into the 'us' and 'them' paradigm. This is the view that our governing class is a thing unto itself, insulated, unapproachable and unassailable.

Reinforcing that is the self-aggrandizing attitude of our elected officials, who from the mere fact that they were legitimately chosen to represent the citizenry through the electoral process, act as though they are a separate and transcendent class, the High Priests of Privilege and Prerogative. They regard themselves as now gifted with powers and insights which are far beyond the grasp of ordinary mortals, thus are to be trusted and left alone as they go about dealing with the complexities of creating new laws which determine the future functioning and direction of the nation.

We, the slobbering masses at the bottom of this power pyramid, are thus left asking a lot of questions: What are "they" doing? What are "they" planning? And maybe the most important one of all: What in the world are "they" spending the money on now?

The insulting reality is, when it comes to government budgeting and spending, except for the mostly empty ritual of voting – only every two years – everyday citizens are never consulted, much less do they ever give their specific consent on vital decisions made in their name. This is a *colossal disconnect* for what is putatively a democracy. Name another activity that comes close in scale to the allocation of trillions of dollars of tax revenue and borrowed shortfalls by federal, state and municipal governments.

To appreciate what an abuse of power this has become, let me throw out some very basic propositions. Please correct me if I'm wrong.

Starting with a question: In a democratic country – government of the people, by the people, for the people – who "owns" the government's money?

Either money is privately owned – people, companies, corporations, investment banks, etc. – or it's publicly owned.

If through taxes, bonds, borrowing, printing, digital creation, money is deposited in the U.S. Treasury for later disbursement, whose money is it? Who actually OWNS that money before it's sent on its way to pay the bills?

Yes, Congress has the power and responsibility to decide where the money goes. The President has some discretion about spending money, as long as such disbursements are "legal", that is, authorized by laws which specify the allocation of said monies and the president's expenditures are not in violation of the Constitution.

But Joe Biden doesn't own it. Neither does Nancy Pelosi or Mitch McConnell or Chuck Schumer. It's not *their* money.

Make no mistake about it, our leaders act as if it's theirs. I mean this in both senses. Sometimes out of some misplaced sense of entitlement and sheer arrogance, these folks do act like the trillions that pass through the U.S. Treasury is their personal slush fund to do with as they see fit.

The other is the strictly legal sense. In specific legal terms, government officials, regardless of how highly placed, are only empowered to act as trustees, to direct the disbursement of those funds, with the general understanding that such spending ultimately serves to serve the general needs of the country, "promote the general welfare", and to enable the functioning of the government, all of the foregoing ON BEHALF OF THE CITIZENRY.

In neither case, however, is the money in fact theirs. As when we deposit money in a bank, the bank may have physical possession of it – whatever that means in a world of digital transactions and bookkeeping – but it's still our money.

So who should we say owns the money the government at any given time has in its coffers?

We could ask a similar question about public property and infrastructure. This might offer some guidance. Who owns the interstate highway system? Who owns the roads, ramps, bridges?

Yes, the obvious answer is the government. But as a democracy, as active participants in a system of self-government, aren't WE the government?

I think there's a common but valid and extremely useful understanding which we should insist on here.

Acknowledging that some have asserted via The Act of 1871[1] there has been a corporate framework, a legal entity – a legalistic sham[2] – set up to accommodate the necessity of our federal government machinery having status and standing in the vast economic environs which we call domestically the national economy, which then participates in the vaster economic environment known as the world economy, I still think the best understanding of "ownership" when it comes to the commons is that WE THE PEOPLE collectively own the physical and financial assets of the United States of America. The CITIZENS. Not those charged with representing the needs, wants and priorities of the citizens, not those doing what needs to be done to realize in real terms what we democratically decide needs to be done – i.e. the Pelosis, McConnells, and Bidens in positions of power. It is WE THE PEOPLE who confer to them the power to act on our behalf, to protect, develop, expand those assets, ON BEHALF OF THE PEOPLE, serving our interests individually and collectively. That assignment of power is not without conditions; assumes transparency and full accountability; is not permanent in the sense that officials of government are not permanent fixtures (bureaucrats tend to be more enduring but certainly elected officials have fixed terms of service); can be withdrawn or withheld, though admittedly this is a cumbersome process; is not unlimited but reflects constitutional as well as statutory limitations, and whatever limits WE THE PEOPLE decide to impose.

It is WE THE PEOPLE who have original and overriding control – ownership? – of what passes through the Treasury and where that money goes. After all, it is OUR tax dollars which are collected and pooled to fund the government, it is in OUR name that bonds are floated and it is US who are directly obligated to repay at some future time the money borrowed to fund the government. It seems reasonable to conclude that until that money is disbursed for whatever reason and is on its way to creditors or the states or government contractors, or paid as salaries to federal employees, or sent to anyone who has a legitimate claim for payment, the money which is in the vaults and accounts of OUR government is OURS.

In an important sense, that money is collectivized, is subject to joint and collective ownership, before it is collected, as it's collected, when it's collected and is sitting in the bank.

This applies to infrastructure and physical assets as well. Granted, we individually have no right to claim a chunk of asphalt from an interstate highway or one of the fingers from the statue of Abraham Lincoln overlooking the Capitol Mall. We collectively own such items and consent to leave it in trust so that we collectively can enjoy our common property, whatever its agreed purpose.

Why should we look at the hard cold cash inside the Treasury vaults or Fort Knox any differently?

On occasion we merely hint at the idea that it's "our money". Usually as submissive supplicants, grateful for some token generosity by our elected officials. For example, with the lockdowns, shutdowns, and shutouts incurred by the overreaction to the Covid-19 "pandemic", it was decided by those we sent to Washington DC to represent our interests – not by them as kings or princesses or queens or Führers – that we would get some Covid-19 relief checks. They were paltry but an example of WE THE PEOPLE benefitting individually as citizens, members of the collective whole, by having some of our money sent back to us from the pool of collectively owned money in the Treasury, as a means of helping us through the crisis.

What is my point?

Citizens cower before the federal government. Yes, it's an awesome and frightening institution. It is massive in size and an imposing, all-encompassing presence in every aspect of our lives. And around the world. The overwhelming temptation is to see it 1) as some frightening, unapproachable, all-powerful, omnipotent behemoth, and often 2) as an adversary, a separate entity, a force to be reckoned with.

It is not necessarily either of these. It's only humbling, intimidating, incapacitating, oppressive, tyrannical, if we decide to view it that way. To regard our government, at least within the theoretical framework of even our highly-compromised democracy, as "them" and we citizens as "us" is a self-fulfilling, self-sabotaging notion and a guarantee that those we do assign stewardship of our public affairs to, most certainly WILL misuse their power, WILL abuse us, WILL act like they "own it", and DO A LOT OF THINGS which are contrary to our interests, if not ultimately destructive to the historic promise made to the world with the founding of our experiment in self-rule.

Does this sound like I'm talking about some abstract principle? The stuff of academic or high-sounding rhetoric but not of the real world?

In practice, the impact of ignoring this idea is far from abstract. There are many very severe real-world consequences.

Our timidity and imagined powerlessness create the monster the federal government has become. Our accepting the false narrative of a two-party system has all but destroyed democracy. Our letting our leaders feed us lies without retribution, in fact our *rewarding* our leaders for misleading and abusing us, is putting nails in our own coffins. Our letting the DOD use us as an ATM machine for endless wars and shopping sprees is bankrupting the country. Our sitting by idly while the Fed prints trillions of dollars and feeds it directly into accounts of the already appallingly rich, our accepting and swallowing the idiotic fairy tales of *Make America Great Again* and *Build Back Better* when these phony grand visions are just more vehicles for the strip mining of our economy and the destruction of the middle class, is immersing us in crippling delusions and willful ignorance. Our electing officials who enable and incentivize the ruin of our industrial and manufacturing base and subsidize the export of good jobs is hiring criminals to rob us. Our willful ignorance about the havoc the U.S. wreaks around the world, creating the immigrant crisis we now face is poisoning us with racist nonsense and blinding us to the class war being waged on us. These and many more habits of laziness, cowardice, and neglect are coming home to roost. The mess we see ourselves in right now with the meltdown of the economy, the health crises (and there are many more beyond Covid-19), and the ongoing conflict with Russia and the coming major confrontation with China, are just previews of coming attractions. This is not going to end well for "we the people".

It's our money.[3]

It's our country.[4]

We better start acting like it.[5]

Personal Debt

Time to make this personal.

Because it is personal!

Let's look at the financial condition of the citizens of our country.

HOME MORTGAGE DEBT: Being a homeowner is certainly central to the American Dream. But what does that mean when the home you "own" is strapped with a mortgage? It means that if you miss successive payments, your ownership will evaporate and your home will become property of the bank you got your home loan from.

Nevertheless, everyday citizens do their best to find a home which, if not a fulfillment of their dreams, meets enough of their needs and expectations, then buy it from funds borrowed from a bank or other home lending institution, paying over the course of a 20 or 30-year mortgage two to three times the price of the house.

This can be a troublesome arrangement, as many homeowners discovered during the 2008 economic crisis. Property values plunged and millions of folks discovered they owed the banks more than their property was worth.

Nevertheless, almost 64% of Americans own their own home,[1] and there are 83.6 million mortgages[2] in the system, averaging $143,674. The total home mortgage debt for the country stands at a record $12.6 trillion,[3] as of the first quarter of 2023, representing 70.4% of all consumer debt.[4] As part of that mortgage debt, "Americans owe $340 billion on 13.1 million home equity lines of credit" – additional borrowing against their homes – averaging $25,974 per loan.

CREDIT CARD DEBT: In the latest numbers from the New York Federal Reserve, consumer credit card debt just made the biggest surge in history.[5] The total outstanding is now $1.03 trillion[6] and the rate of growth shows no signs of slowing. Recent increases in inflation[7] have taken a toll on consumers. People are not only finding it difficult to buy what they need but are having difficulty making

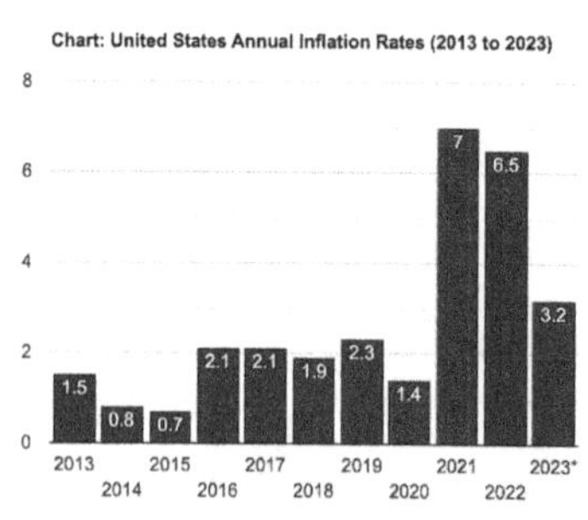

card payments on time. "The latest data also showed that the rate of households becoming delinquent or entering serious delinquency (behind by 90 days or more) on their credit cards was the highest since the end of 2011."[8]

AUTOMOTIVE DEBT: At $1.55 trillion, automotive debt represents 9.17% of all consumer debt.[9] Americans have little choice in the matter. Public transportation is minimal, too often not available at all. If they have a job and want to go to work, they drive, demanding a huge chunk of the family budget. In the first quarter of 2023,[10] the average car payment for a new vehicle was $725 per month, used vehicles $516, leases coming in at $586 per month. As with credit card debt, delinquencies were on the rise, with 6.1% of auto loan buyers are currently behind[11] on payments.

STUDENT LOAN DEBT: As discussed before, currently there is a total of $1.75 trillion outstanding[12] on over 60.4 million student loans, affecting over 1 in 5 American adults.

OTHER DEBT: Other debt mainly consists of medical debt and personal loans. Over 19.5 million Americans have personal loans averaging $18,255 totaling $356 billion.[13] Over 23 million – that's 9% of the adult population[14] – owe medical debt. "Out of these, 11 million had balances greater than $2,000, and 3 million owed more than $10,000." The Consumer Financial Protection Board puts the total for medical debt at $88 billion.[15]

Add it up: U.S. citizens are personally in debt over $17.3 trillion!

Americans, like their government, are in hock up to their eyebrows. You have to wonder, what kind of country do we have where nearly 40% if its citizens can't come up with $400 to cover an emergency?[16] Or where people have to put basic food items for the family on a Visa card?[17]

Answer: The kind of country that's perpetually at war. The kind of country which puts military conquest and hegemonic control of the entire globe ahead of the welfare of its citizens.

Though we are constantly steered away from viewing it this way, again let's look to the wisdom of Dwight D. Eisenhower:

> "Every gun that is made, every warship launched, every rocket fired signifies, in the final sense a theft from those who hunger and are not fed, those who are cold and are not clothed. This world in arms is not spending money alone. It is spending the sweat of its laborers, the genius of its scientists, the hopes of its children."

Let's take this even further … we must confront the reality of this insanity.

All of the money spent on unnecessary wars and unneeded military junk, on building bases across the planet and weapons in space, on developing more usable nuclear weapons and sponsoring proxy wars, overthrowing other governments and positioning the U.S. as the great conquering ruler of the planet, all of these antics and blunders and reckless misadventures built around twisted priorities, are visits to the doctor that can't be made, holes in the roof that can't be repaired, they are the bald tires or the car that won't start, the kids' threadbare clothes and old sneakers, the defaulted mortgages and overdue credit card payments, they are the empty bank accounts and empty wallets of millions of citizens who work hard and walk the straight and true but simply can't get ahead, who find themselves constantly falling behind. Trillions and trillions of dollars withheld or taken from citizens, real people living real lives, only to create chaos in the world, to inflict death and destruction on other countries, to create animus and hostility toward the U.S., to turn potential partners and allies into enemies, dollar by dollar stolen from individuals and families and neighborhoods and communities which are slipping slowly and inevitably deeper into poverty and desperation.

Those big numbers with their strings of zeroes may look impressive, even elegant, as they line up in pretty columns on a spreadsheet. But they are much more than just arithmetic symbols. Those big numbers down on the ground represent pain and frustration, broken dreams, defeat and lost opportunities. They equate to hunger pangs and hopelessness. They represent the futures of real life people being compromised and destroyed.

Let's review.

The Korean War to stop the post-WWII communist surge was a failure and cost the U.S. 36,574 dead and $389 billion up in smoke.

The Vietnam War to again halt the communist surge was a failure and cost the U.S. 57,979 dead and $840 billion.

The first Iraq war, while it resulted in a minimum loss of American life, was still a failure and racked up a price tag of $102 billion.[18]

Again, the Brown University Costs of War Project[19]: "Through Fiscal Year 2022, the United States federal government has spent and obligated $8 trillion dollars on the post-9/11 wars in Afghanistan, Pakistan, Iraq and elsewhere."

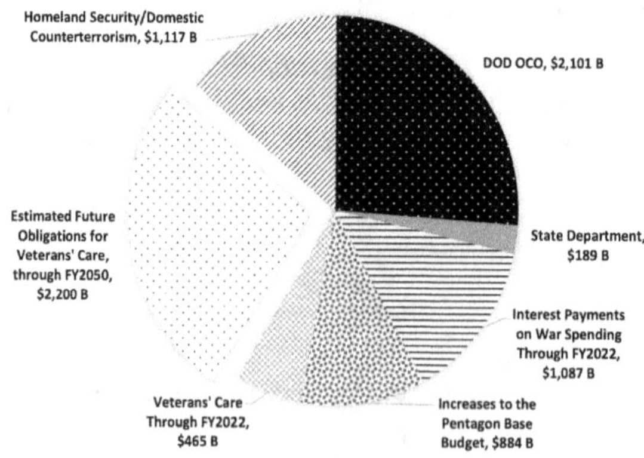

$8 TRILLION DOLLARS!

That's one of those "big money" numbers that is impossible to wrap our heads around. Let's unpack it.

$8 trillion is $23,825 for each and every person in America! Young, old, fat, thin, white, black, Latina. Every person. For a family of four, that's over $95,000 either collected in taxes or borrowed against their future, a debt burden likewise borne by each and every one of us. It's a big hole in the family budget, money stolen from us for completely pointless wars.

Then there's the bloated defense budgets. In 1992 with the breakup of the Soviet Union, our Cold War adversary of the previous four decades disappeared. We could now hold the line on defense spending, even reduce it. We were promised a "peace dividend". Tragically, after seven years of slight reductions 1993-2000, defense spending substantially increased. The DOD budget in 1992 was $325 billion,[20] the second highest since WWII, only exceeded by $100 million in 1990. The official defense budget for 2023 at $816.7 billion was more than double that. Though $325 billion was a very generous figure at the time, if we use the 1992 budget as a baseline – 1992 being the year the Soviet Union collapsed, thus the last year the U.S. was confronted by a major military power – and reason there was and is no necessity for the DOD requiring more than that amount to keep America safe, we can get some idea how skewed our nation's priorities have gotten. The total amount of budget excess, that is, DOD budgeting that exceeded the $325 billion of 1992, from 1993 to present totals a jaw-dropping ... *$7.18 trillion!*

And then there's the bloated budgets of two other organizations central to maintaining full spectrum dominance[21] by the U.S. military worldwide, and conducting the War On Terror against our new 9/11-spawned enemies.

Since 9/11, special ops – mostly operating in the "black" world of espionage and regime change – by the CIA/NSA have squandered another $354.7 billion.

Since 9/11, under the disingenuous cover of protecting Americans by conducting a War on Terror right here, within our own borders, the Department of Homeland Security has wasted yet another $232.5 billion.

There are other equally wasteful defense-related expenditures tucked away in the dark recesses of agency and departmental budgets. But the above captures the most egregious abuses.

There are two vitally important points we need to remember.

First, *none of the military expansion subsequent to the disappearance of the USSR was and is necessary.* The U.S. spends more

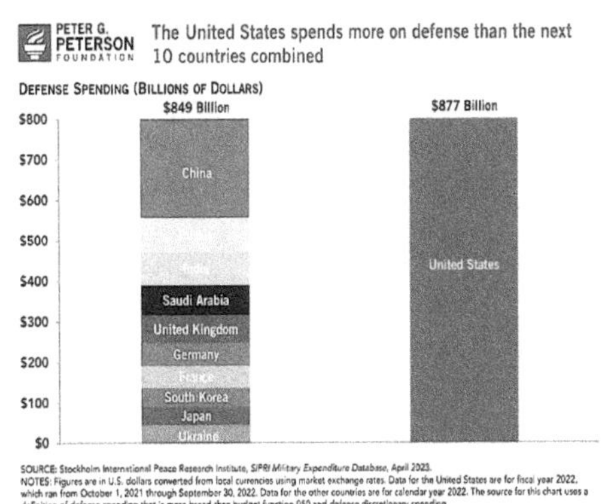

SOURCE: Stockholm International Peace Research Institute, *SIPRI Military Expenditure Database, April 2023.*
NOTES: Figures are in U.S. dollars converted from local currencies using market exchange rates. Data for the United States are for fiscal year 2022, which ran from October 1, 2021 through September 30, 2022. Data for the other countries are for calendar year 2022. The source for this chart uses a definition of defense spending that is more broad than budget function 050 and defense discretionary spending.

on its military than the next ten countries combined. Defense spending is eating up over half of the discretionary spending of the federal government. Both major parties support this. The result is a nation on the brink of bankruptcy and the vital, pressing needs of a citizenry being ignored.

Second, *none of the wars since WWII had to be fought*. Every one of them was a war of choice, driven by an agenda hidden from the public, often even hidden from our elected representatives. All those wars were sold to the public by a web of propaganda and outright lies.

When we add it all up, it represents the most colossal fraud in the history of humankind. Yes, FRAUD! Trillions of our tax dollars taken from us as good, decent citizens under false pretenses, then used to fight unnecessary wars and buy military junk we never needed. Money which just ends up in the coffers of the defense industry, and ultimately in the bank accounts of wealthy investors who profit from the never-ending wars. It's a pipeline right from the pocketbooks of everyday citizens and their meager family budgets, to the already incomprehensibly rich.

This is *our* tax dollars making a mess of the world and piling up tens of thousands of corpses, often innocent people who were no more to blame than you or your next-door neighbor for the trouble in the world.

This is money which you and I could have put to much better use, feeding and caring for our loved ones, laying the foundation for a healthier, happier citizenry and a future that offers a better world for all of us.

The Systemic Poison Pill

I hope we now can appreciate the scope and scale of the "debt trap" that is destroying our nation, an epic tragedy unfolding in slow motion which will ultimately end the prospects and hopes of future citizens, consigning the American Dream to the septic tank of history.

To find a way out of the seemingly inevitable catastrophe, to look for an escape from this road to ruin, we must come full circle and stare down the obvious question we began with.

How does the federal government of the allegedly richest, most powerful nation in history end up saddling itself with more than \$34 trillion in debt?[1] Why does the U.S. have to borrow money if it's so wealthy?

The answer is as obvious as it is infuriating.

Those who are running the show have no common sense, fiscal discipline, wisdom or prudence. Everything is subordinate to imposing Pax Americana empire on the rest of the world. Our leaders are drunk on power, delusional, myopic, detached from reality, and poisoned by exceptionalism – the extreme, fanatical, and completely unsupportable proposition that America is the "exceptional" nation, chosen by destiny to lead the rest of humankind, whose subordination and inferiority are presumed as a given – thus the U.S. is deemed by divine right to rule as absolute, indisputable, infallible hegemon.

But it goes beyond that.

And still leaves open the question …

Why so much debt? On the surface, it's quite simple.

The federal government spends more than it takes in as revenues. Congress, to please its deep-pocketed donors – the ones who fund their expensive campaigns and keep them returning to their cushy jobs in Washington – keeps personal taxes on them and their business interests extremely low, keeps their corporations on the short list for subsidies and lucrative government contracts, and looks the other way when vast amounts of privately held wealth are off-shored, thus beyond the reach of the IRS.

However! There's a much more profound reason: *our systemic poison pill!* The U.S. has a flawed economic system, one that will self-destruct over the long haul. It's time to face a harsh reality. Debt-based issuance of currency – borrowing money at interest to inject it into the economy – is a Ponzi scheme.[2] End of story. It is fraud perpetrated on an international scale, since almost 30% of America's public debt is foreign owned.[3] Borrowing money at interest to create more money is a bargain with the Devil. The borrowed money can never be paid back. Moreover, each tranche of new borrowing devalues the money already in circulation. Only the investor class benefits in the short run via speculation, while the rest of the population – a huge majority – are left holding the bag of increasingly worthless promissory notes. Yes, each chunk of cash, whether a digital entry or hard currency is essentially a "promise" that said chunk will be honored at its declared value, whatever "honored" means that's predicated on the full faith and credit of the United States of America. The assurance that you can "take that to the bank" assumes the bank will forever be open and solvent. The current deficit of more than $34 trillion, the rate at which it's growing accelerating, driving an annual debt service of over $1 trillion[4] – that's the interest we're paying on what's *already* owed – doesn't inspire much confidence in the "full faith and credit of the U.S." It shouldn't. In terms of serving the needs of the citizenry, that $1+ trillion interest is much-needed cash that goes up in smoke as, or more accurately, into the bank accounts of the already extremely well off. The need to increase interest rates to combat inflation[5] will dramatically exacerbate this debt service catastrophe.

All of this is a gigantic red flag waving over our economy, which the rest of the world is increasingly taking note of. Add to that the humiliating high drama of the congressional debt ceiling battles and the recurring threat of government shutdowns[6] – viewed worldwide with shock and disbelief – it's clear that if we stay the present course, our days as the economic gorilla in the room and world power are numbered.

However, stating the problem so unambiguously is a far cry from being able to properly address such a deeply entrenched paradigm, regardless of how insanely wrong and self-destructive it is. The truth is, everyday citizens mostly aren't paying attention, thus aren't aware of any of this. And we certainly can't rely on those in power who benefit from the current arrangement to fix the mess. They're making a killing on it and as long as it remains in place, we can only count on the current beneficiaries of the system as now configured to extract every bit of wealth from our skewed, rigged economy, until it finally goes belly up. This privileged elite will continue to live in splendor in well-guarded underground bunkers, or have Elon Musk rocket them to colonies on the Moon or Mars.

• • •

Despite such a bleak assessment, make no mistake about it: There is a way out of this mess. It only requires some sanity and a sober, clear-minded look at the Constitution, rather modest demands which sadly fail to move our current batch of elected officials. The Constitution without nuance or caveat states:

> The Congress shall have Power To lay and collect Taxes, Duties, Imposts and Excises, to pay the Debts and provide for the common Defence and general Welfare of the United States; but all Duties, Imposts and Excises shall be uniform throughout the United States; To borrow money on the credit of the United States; To regulate Commerce with foreign Nations, and among the several States, and with the Indian Tribes; To coin Money, regulate the Value thereof …

This could not be clearer: If the economy requires money in circulation, Congress has the power to coin – or print – such instruments, whether as a metallic object or script. No need to borrow. Fire up the smelters or the printing presses. The required currency is created, and the need is met.

Under pressure from the banking sector – both national and international – with the Federal Reserve Act,[7] our government in 1913 ceded that power to a private banking institution, the Federal Reserve. Woodrow Wilson, who signed the act into law later expressed his regret.

> *"I am a most unhappy man. I have unwittingly ruined my country. A great industrial nation is controlled by its system of credit. Our system of credit is concentrated. The growth of the nation, therefore, and all our activities are in the hands of a few men. We have come to be one of the worst ruled, one of the most completely controlled and dominated Governments in the civilized world - no longer a Government by free opinion, no longer a Government by conviction and the vote of the majority, but a Government by the opinion and duress of a small group of dominant men."*

But here is the reality: What can be done – what is done – can be undone. Again, we cannot expect those now in power to act. They are too thoroughly in the pockets of the ruling elite, who are generously rewarded by the status quo. We must look to an entirely new batch of legislators, a new Congress, a "people's Congress" to stop the poisoning of our entire economy with debt-based issuance of currency.

• • •

Let me make this absolutely crystal clear, so there's no misunderstanding: We are borrowing money to expand the money supply. Then we borrow money to pay interest on the money we already borrowed.

Which makes me wonder exactly what it is we celebrate on July 4th. Independence? What independence? The U.S. effectively traded its debt and tax slavery to England with debt slavery to a private banking system which is transnational and disavows any loyalty to America as a nation or its citizens.

The only way to end a Ponzi scheme is to end it. Yes, those on the most recent tiers of speculation – and buying U.S. bonds is in the final analysis a form of speculation – will get screwed. They should have invested more wisely. Buying more promissory notes from a government which can't pay back the $34+ trillion it already owes without more borrowing, is sheer stupidity. Tough luck, guys.

Our debt-based currency creation is a rip-off, pure and simple. Ending it is like kicking a heroin habit. You don't end heroin addiction by giving the addict increasing doses of heroin. You cut off the heroin.

I apologize for resorting to common sense.

Yes …

End the Ponzi scheme immediately! This should be among the first orders of business for a people's Congress. Obey the letter of the Constitution. Honor the wisdom and intent of the Founding Fathers.

Just do it!

Peace Dollars: A Modest Beginning

What I'm about to propose is one component of a comprehensive strategy for removing the warmongers from power who are driving our country to its destruction. The entire approach will be presented in total in the final book of this series: *The Art of War, The Science of Peace.*

While a critical part of a broad-ranging, game-changing, paradigm-shifting proposal, it can function as a standalone force for change, a modest beginning in the dramatic new trajectory required for deep, profound systemic reform – a renewal of the core values upon which our nation was founded.

I call the idea Peace Dollars. As the name implies, it is the utilization of our most basic monetary instrument, specifically for the promotion of peace.

First, some background.

Special use currency is not unprecedented.

Abraham Lincoln used "greenbacks" – the paper currency shown below – backed by nothing more than confidence in the government – to finance the Civil War. He printed $449,338,902 of this currency, a lot of money at the time.

Then, a century later, on June 4, 1963, John F. Kennedy signed Executive Order 11110 which set in motion the issuance of silver certificate notes, currency backed by silver reserves being held at that time by the U.S. Treasury.

Records show that Kennedy initially issued $4,292,893,825 worth of cash money. This bypassed the established procedure of borrowing money into circulation from the Federal Reserve. $20 billion of such United States Notes were eventually put into circulation before he was assassinated. It has been suggested it was Kennedy's and Lincoln's introduction of such interest-free, debt-free currency which was the reason both of them were murdered.[1]

Understand that, as pointed out before, their actions were completely within the framework of the Constitution. Presidents must seek Congressional approval, as the ultimate authority for creating money properly resides with Congress, as delineated in Article 1: The Legislative Branch, Section 8: Powers of Congress.

There is no question that what both Lincoln and Kennedy did, while anathema to private banking interests, was entirely legal. In fact, progressive economists would argue that money creation never should have been ceded to the private banks[2] in the first place, moreover, that it is incumbent on our current elected officials to again secure absolute control of the currency.[3]

Risk of assassination aside, no legal case or compelling argument can be made against using this power. Our current debt-driven system requiring us to borrow from the private banking institution misleadingly named The Federal Reserve, in order to inject money into the economy, is absurd and over the long term counter-productive.

While ultimately our goal should arguably be to totally eliminate the Federal Reserve's role in this process, at least for now we can pick up where Kennedy left off, prudently using what we call *U.S. Peace Dollars*, to cover a sizable portion of the federal government's budgeting requirements.

U.S. Peace Dollars would look almost exactly like their Federal Reserve Note counterparts. Same layout, same denominations, same founders-of-the-nation and presidential images. Where U.S. currency now says …

FEDERAL RESERVE NOTE

… *U.S. Peace Dollars* not surprisingly would say …

U. S. PEACE DOLLARS

Where U.S. currency now says …

IN GOD WE TRUST

… *U.S. Peace Dollars* would say …

PROMOTING PEACE

Where in nearly microscopic print U.S. currency now says …

THIS NOTE IS LEGAL TENDER FOR
ALL DEBTS, PUBLIC AND PRIVATE

… *U.S. Peace Dollars* would say …

THIS NOTE IS LEGAL TENDER FOR ALL DOMESTIC
FINANCIAL TRANSACTIONS, PUBLIC AND PRIVATE

Which brings up a critical feature of this financial instrument: *U.S. Peace Dollars* would be for domestic use only! This is to prevent them from being shipped overseas or being fed into the ongoing frenzy of currency speculation. Banks would be instructed to block the transfer of *U.S. Peace Dollars* equivalencies to non-domestic banking institutions.

For example, if a person deposited $8,000 of *U.S. Peace Dollars* into a domestic account, transfer of funds to non-domestic banks or use of funds for purchases outside the U.S. could only be made from balances of his or her account in excess of $8,000 accruing from regular Federal Reserve Note deposits.

This restriction is to guarantee that *U.S. Peace Dollars* exclusively promote America's <u>*domestic economy*</u>, meaning only purchasing goods and services "Made in the USA". This precludes exporting any newly generated Peace Dividend wealth, which would only exacerbate our already excessive trade deficit and facilitate capital flight from the country.

Private banks would be incentivized to create *U.S. Peace Dollars* credit cards. If there is institutional resistance to this by private banks, the U.S. government can fill that need by issuing through its own agencies such credit instruments.

A host of small-business and employee-owned business incentives could be built around *U.S. Peace Dollars*, for example giving matching federal grants or at least preferential treatment for investing *U.S. Peace Dollars* in job-creating domestic business start-ups. Worker-owned businesses, co-ops, and sole proprietorships could be high on the priority list for such support.

All of this points the economy in a hopeful and highly constructive, new direction. Further expanding general usage of *U.S. Peace Dollars* down the road could gradually dismantle the current Debt Doomsday Machine of the Federal Reserve paradigm. We could begin to wind down our $34+ trillion dollar deficit and balance the annual federal budgets using *U.S. Peace Dollars* to fill in the gap between tax revenue and overall spending.

Imagine Congress arguing over the size of budget *surpluses* instead of budget deficits!

Wouldn't that be refreshing?

Lincoln was a Republican and Kennedy was a Democrat. Do party labels really matter when a person is doing good things for the people?

The point is, there are actionable solutions to our problems, even those deep systemic flaws in our system. But we have to act and we have to start somewhere. Peace Dollars is one small but positive step in unraveling the web of debt which shrouds our economy and makes access to a fair share of the enormous wealth of our nation impossible for the vast majority of citizens.

People need to wake up, yes. But they need concrete steps to take when they realize how rigged the system is and how it is entirely on their shoulders to do something about it.

U.S. Peace Dollars represent just such a concrete step.

We the people need to take a stand and stand our ground. We the people need to inaugurate genuine alternatives to the status quo. We can do that by introducing real choice at the polls, i.e. finding individuals who will support innovations like the Peace Dollar initiative, getting them on the ballot, and replacing in elected positions our current lapdogs to the ruling elite with such individuals …

Candidates of the people, by the people, for the people.

True representative democracy!

There is no other way.

A Nation at Peace

To a hammer, everything looks like a nail.

To a warmonger, every problem calls for a war.

WAR! WAR! WAR!

FOREVER WAR! UNENDING WAR!

Our current leaders are hypnotized by war. They lack the vision and resourcefulness to consider negotiation and cooperation. Peace is not in their thoughts. 'Peace' is not in their vocabulary. They are addicted to war. They are *obsessed with war.*

The lesson we must take from this is this: Talking to them, trying to change their minds, trying to alter their policies and methods, is a COMPLETE WASTE OF TIME. It's like yelling at storm clouds and telling them to stop raining. It's like trying to convince a desert to stop being so hot and dry. It's like talking to a wall and expecting a reply.

Which means, there is only one sensible, rational, effective course of action …

Current U.S. leadership, at all levels — we're probably looking at 99% of those now in positions of power — MUST BE REPLACED.

This is the only possible way to stop U.S. aggression and wanton promotion of chaos and violence in the world.

This MUST BE THE ENTIRE FOCUS OF PEACE ACTIVISM going forward. We have no choice in the matter. The record is clear — an unblemished record of total failure to stop, or even slow down, the war machine — an unblemished record of total failure to stop, or even slow down, the war machine.

Make no mistake about it! Replacing these misfits, psychopaths, sociopaths, and enemies of peace now in power, will not be easy.

But it can — and must — be done!

Our survival as a nation, perhaps the survival of the entire human race is at stake!

Here's what it will take.

The two major parties will not give us the choices we need to make. Both the Republicans and Democrats are in the pockets of the military-industrial complex. And to bolster their commitment to this vast money laundering enterprise, where hundreds of billions of dollars end up in the coffers of giant defense companies and ultimately into the bank accounts of the ultra-wealthy, both major parties are fanatically committed to making the U.S. an empire.

If we want peace, we will have to elect peace candidates. And to elect peace candidates, we must on our own initiative put peace candidates on the ballot.

Identifying and choosing excellent alternatives to the pro-war establishment candidates will not be complicated. We have at our disposal a litmus test, consisting of three questions to be put to prospective candidates:

Prospective Peace Candidate . . .

1) **Will you fully support legislation to reduce the total DOD/military budget by 33-50%?**

2) **Will you fully support legislation to reverse U.S. intimidation and aggressive posturing toward other nations?**

3) **Will you fully support legislation to introduce Peace Dollars as a domestic-use-only legal currency?**

If a candidate answers 'yes' to all three, he or she deserves our full support and our vote. We then do everything it takes to get this person on the ballot. There are three ways to get them on the ballot:

First option is to use primaries. That is, run them in the next primary against one of the major party candidates.

Second option is to run the candidates as "third party", e.g. as a Green or Libertarian or other minor party candidate.

Third option is to put them on the ballot as an independent.

Whatever strategy we adopt certainly will require some serious dedication and hard work. We'll have to organize locally and talk to voters face-to-face, badger local media for news coverage. We'll have to organized rallies and bake sales, visit churches, convalescent homes, community clubs and organizations.

But recognize . . . THIS IS DEMOCRACY AT ITS BEST!

It is citizens, locally, community-by-community, working together to signal their priorities, put their values before the public, and introduce REAL CHOICE at the polls.

Once peace candidates are on the ballot, then it's up to the voting public. If we the people want to end the wars, reverse the rampant militarization of our society, if we truly want peace, then ...

WE ONLY VOTE FOR PEACE CANDIDATES!

It's that simple.

This is how we "fire" the warmongers who now populate the halls of Congress and other seats of power.

This is how we stop the squandering of our national wealth, the theft of *our money!*

This is how we inaugurate A NATION AT PEACE!
And guess what?
The whole world will thank us!

Closing Editorial Comments

Let's not delude ourselves.

America has big problems.

And . . .

Big problems require big solutions. Bold solutions. Innovative thinking. Not tinkering around the edges.

It all seems so overwhelming because it is overwhelming.

The sheer magnitude of the problems means an enormous potential for catastrophe if we don't get it right.

Plus, we are being overwhelmed – maybe 'inundated' is a better choice of words – by the 24/7 media tsunami of distractions. Crises, disasters, scandals, most of which, while spectacular and riveting, makes it all but impossible to think clearly, get some perspective, even achieve a basic grasp of what any of it means, where all of this is going, and in particular, what are the root problems, the essential core items we truly need to be paying attention to.

Overall, the biggest distractions come from our politicians. And yes, it's intentional. Or at the very least, wired into them. If they gave straight answers, they wouldn't be in power. That's the way the system works now. One of the things that must change.

So, confusion, obfuscation, disinformation, unreality reigns.

The way around this is to ask ourselves: What kind of America do we want? What needs to be done to make that America a reality?

Most Americans can give a fairly straightforward answer to these questions. They are real people living real lives in real time. They know what challenges they face getting from one day to the next.

I've looked at polls for two decades now. Unsurprisingly, the priorities of most U.S. citizens[1] have varied rather little. Let's review what everyday citizens right now say is important to them.

> 74% of Americans want a federal minimum wage of $20.00 per hour.
>
> 86% of voters want fair trade agreements protecting jobs, workers, the environment.
>
> 69% of voters want a public option which provides truly affordable, universal health care, and/or Medicar-4-All.
>
> 88% of voters want no reductions in Social Security; 82% of voters support expanding it.
>
> 72% of voters are dissatisfied with current policies to reduce or control crime.

61% of voters want a cut back on military spending.

80% of voters oppose the "Citizens United" U.S. Supreme Court decision.

67% of voters think taxes on the wealthy should be increased.

69% of voters think corporations should be required to pay their fair share in taxes.

83% of voters support massive infrastructure repair, renewal and upgrading.

65% of voters want laws to combat climate change.

65% of voters want tuition free at public colleges and universities.

84% of voters believe valid photo ID should be required to vote. 63% of voters want the president elected by popular vote. 71% of voters want early voting to be made easier. 75% of voters want early voting to be held for two weeks. 74% of voters want election day to be an official legal holiday. 65% of voters support same day voter registration.

I think it's obvious why none of this gets done. It's money. Big money in politics is destroying our democracy. Which translates to: Those in power are not doing their job. Their job is working for us, the people who vote them into their prestigious, extremely cushy jobs in our nation's capital. Listening to us, understanding us, embracing our values and priorities, then creating laws which enable and implement the vision of the America we want. What else could government of the people, by the people, for the people possibly mean?

Whether or not those in power understand this and are intentionally ignoring their real responsibility to THE PEOPLE, is academic. They're not doing their job!

Which leaves us no other option than replacing them … ALL OF THEM!

This seemingly unbreachable chasm between the people and the politicos is no better illustrated than the obsession with the military and the endless wars.

'War is making us poor!' is not just a catchy meme.

It's FACT! It's a big, bold, unmistakable fact. It's the big fat elephant in the room.

It's such a humungous, scary, destructive elephant that I believe it represents the "Achilles heel" of the entire Machiavellian edifice which needs to come down before we can make any progress on the myriad of issues which need the attention of a "people's White House and Congress", policies which genuinely serve all Americans – not just the MIC, the Deep State, Wall Street, not just investment banks, hedge funds, the oligarchs –

and will put our country back on track to becoming a functioning democracy again.

Politicians from both major parties compete for bragging rights on promoting wars and expanding the military. No one in or campaigning for public office dares to risk being accused of being weak on defense. It's who can be the toughest, shout the loudest, make the most convincing threats, against both our alleged enemies and sometimes even our allies.

It's an orgy of advocated violence, wrapped in the flag, juiced up with media-friendly slogans, battle cries, and virtue signaling. Some slither into the national conversations by being more subtle …

Honor the flag!
Support our troops!
Protect the homeland!

… others more overtly aggressive …

Stop China!
Expand NATO
Sanction Russia!

… the sinister ones being combative and confrontational …

Bomb Syria!
Destroy Russia!
Kill Vladimir Putin!
Send troops to Ukraine!
Give more weapons to Taiwan!

No longer do we ever hear any serious mention of, much less advocacy for peace. Diplomacy and negotiation are off the table. No attempts are made to hide or mask our bullying and belligerence. It's our way or bombs away.

Yet, despite the 24/7 saber rattling from officials in high places, mirrored and amplified by a media which acts as the propaganda arm of the DOD, State Department, CIA, NSA, and other Deep State institutions, it's clear that most citizens do not want military conflict. Julian Assange puts it brilliantly …

> *"I've discovered that nearly every war that has started in the past 50 years has been a result of media lies. The media could have stopped it if they'd search deep enough. If they hadn't reprinted government propaganda, they could have stopped it. But what does that mean? Well, that means populations don't like wars. And populations have to be fooled into wars. Populations don't willingly with open eyes go into war. So if we have a good media environment, then you will also have a peaceful environment. Our number one enemy is ignorance."*

Thus, the warrior state creates a tsunami of distortions, disinformation, propaganda and lies, and the public is bounced around from one crisis to the next, never able to get its bearings, never really able to grasp fully the big picture, not able to get answers because it doesn't even know what questions to ask, and certainly is never able to mount a challenge to the military madness that now drives all our policy decisions and defines America's place in the world.

Now imagine. In this swirling firestorm of anxiety, apprehension, fear, intimidation, belligerence and bullying, which is the current manufactured "reality", there are still a significant number of hopeful, determined activists who don't for a moment buy the endless war narrative, and with noble optimism and inspiring dedication promote the idea that the U.S. can and should get along with other countries, in fact, lead the world toward more stable, harmonious, and peaceful coexistence.

You've heard their appeals …

No blood for oil!
Books Not Bombs
Close Guantanamo!
No Weapons in Space
Bring the troops home!
End the War in Ukraine!
'NO' to NATO Expansion

But there's a problem.

These sensible, constructive, forward-looking appeals are directed at the very people who create the false necessity of forever war, who intentionally as a matter of policy make enemies of other nations, who not only believe within their own twisted world view and convoluted political priorities that war is the answer to every question and challenge, but who are *incentivized to promote war*. They and their powerful patrons earn grotesquely huge amounts of money from war and maintain their positions of power by keeping the US on a permanent war footing. These are the predatory, profit-and-power-seeking madmen we beseech to stop what they're doing and end the violence. These are the delusional forever-war militarists we try to reason with, who we attempt to convince to do the "right thing" and start working for a kinder, gentler world.

It's like asking a psychopathic serial killer to stop stabbing so much and start being nice. It's like asking Mike Tyson at the peak of his career when he was 36-0, the youngest heavyweight champion in history, making over $20 million per fight, to stop punching people because hitting people is wrong.

Those now in power will stop nothing short of total world domination.

They think the U.S. is "indispensable", "exceptional" – i.e. above the law.

63

They claim the U.S. is chosen by destiny to rule over all of humankind.
They evidently think because of their high positions, they're infallible.
Yes, our national leaders are delusional, arguably insane.
But so are we, if we think for an instant they're listening to us!
It's time to stop kidding ourselves!
It's time to take a deep breath and look at reality.
It's time to face the ugly truth of what we're up against.
It's time to understand our enemies and what it will take to stop them.

If you take nothing else away from this book you now hold in your hands, it is absolutely crucial that you fully embrace these two profound and essential truths. They are vital and urgent.

First ...

War is making us poor!
War is destroying us as a people.
War is bankrupting our country politically,
spiritually, socially, and economically.

Second ...

Peace is not possible without ousting and
replacing the power-drunk, empire-building,
war-crazed lunatics now in control of our
foreign policy and military institutions.

The current U.S. obsession with incessant and apparently limitless military expansion in tandem with the equally untenable goal of total world domination is a malignant psychosis which must be eradicated at every level, in every layer, in every sector and branch of government. We are talking regime change in Washington DC!

This necessity is so obvious, yet right now it's hiding in plain sight.

It must be brought to the forefront. It must be the main topic of the national conversation going forward. THAT is what the "new peace movement" will look like. THAT is what we as activists are tasked to do!

No, it's not going to be easy. But this is our challenge.

This is our essential task, our existential assignment, our marching orders, if we are to prevent WWIII and possible nuclear annihilation.

Is there a more worthy goal?

Is there a more critical mission?

How we engage and galvanize at least 200,000,000 citizens with this message, and finally put power back in the hands of the people, will be the subject of the last volume in this series: *The Art of War, The Science of Peace.*

Notes

Foreword Commentary

1 – Brown University, Watson Institute, Costs of War Project,
    https://watson.brown.edu/costsofwar/#:~:text=An%20estimated%203.6
    %2D3.8%20million,war%20refugees%20and%20displaced%20persons.
2 – Mike Stone, Reuters, March 14, 2023, https://www.reuters.com/world/us/
    biden-wants-886-billion-defense-ukraine-continues-china-looms-2023-03-
    13/.

Author's Introduction

1 – Zachary B. Wolf, CNN, September 21, 2023, https://edition.cnn.com/2023/
    09/21/politics/war-funding-ukraine-what-matters/index.html.
2 – Carter C. Price and Kathryn A. Edwards, Rand Corporation,
    https://www.rand. org/ pubs/working_papers/ WRA516-1.html.
3 – Aimee Picchi, CBS News Moneywatch, https://www.cbsnews.com/news/
    billionaires-pandemic-1-trillion-wealth-gain/.
4 – *Sheldon S. Walin, Princeton University Press,* Democracy Incorporated:
    Managed Democracy and the Specter of Inverted Totalitarianism,
    *https://press.princeton.edu/books/paperback/9780691178486/democracy-
    incorporated*
5 – Martin Gilens and Benjamin I. Page, "Testing Theories of American Politics:
    Elites, Interest Groups, and Average Citizens", https://www.cambridge.org/
    core/journals/perspectives-on-politics/article/testing-theories-of-american-
    politics-elites-interest-groups-and-average-citizens/62327F513959D0A304
    D4893B382B992B

Numbers of Scale

1 – Robin Scher, Nation of Change, July 12, 2023, https://www.nationofchange.
    org/2023/07/12/the-impact-of-plastic-on-human-health/.
2 – "The Great Pacific Garbage Patch", https://theoceancleanup.com/great-
    pacific-garbage-patch/.

Big Money

1 – Wikipedia, "The Millionaire (TV Series)", https://en.wikipedia.org/wiki/The_
    Millionaire_(TV_series).
2 – Soo Youn, ABC News, May 25, 2019, https://abcnews.go.com/US/10-
    americans-struggle-cover-400-emergency-expense-federal/story?id
    =63253846.
3 – Annie Massa and Jack Witzig, Bloomberg, July 4, 2023,
    https://www.bloomberg.com/news/articles/2023-07-03/musk-zuckerberg-
    lead-852-billion-wealth-surge-among-world-rich.

Brown University's Cost of War Project

1 – Website of Brown University's Watson Institute Cost of War project, https://watson.brown.edu/costsofwar/.
2 – Peace Dividend Project,"What Is the Peace Dividend Strategy", https://peacedividend.us/what-is-the-peace-dividend-strategy/.
3 – Wikipedia, "Omnibus spending bill", https://en.wikipedia.org/wiki/Omnibus_spending_bill.
4 – Wikipedia, "National Defense Authorization Act", https://en.wikipedia.org/wiki/National_Defense_ Authorization_Act.

More Bases More Bombs More War

1 – Muhammed Hussein and Muhammed Haddad, Aljazeera, September 10, 2021, "Infographic: US military presence around the world", https://www.aljazeera.com/news/2021/9/10/infographic-us-military-presence-around-the-world-interactive.
2 – Conor Friedersdorf, The Atlantic, January 9, 2014, https://www.theatlantic.com/international/archive/2014/01/ the-wedding-that-a-us-drone-strike-turned-into-a-funeral/282936/.

Federal Debt

1 – Hanna Ziady and Tammy Luhby, CNN, "US national debt hits record $34 trillion", January 3, 2024, https://edition.cnn.com/2024/01/03/economy/us-national-debt-34-trillion/index.html.
2 – Emma Taggart, My Modern Met, February 4, 2021 https://mymodernmet.com/modern-rube-goldberg-machine/.
3 – Noah Kirsch, Forbes, November 9, 2017, https://www.forbes.com/sites/ noahkirsch/2017/11/09/the-3-richest-americans-hold-more-wealth-than-bottom-50-of-country-study-finds/.
4 – Wikipedia, "World economy", https://en.wikipedia.org/wiki/World_economy.
5 – Matthew Desmond, *Poverty, by America*, Penguin Random House, https://www.penguinrandomhouse.com/books/675683/poverty-by-america-by-matthew-desmond/.
6 – Brown University's Watson Institute Cost of War Project, "Estimate of U.S. post-911 War Spending, FY2001-2022", https://watson.brown.edu/costsofwar/ figures/2021/BudgetaryCosts.
7 – Brown University's Watson Institute Cost of War Project, "Afghan Civilians", https://watson.brown.edu/costsofwar/costs/human/civilians/afghan.
8 – Samantha Lock, Newsweek, August 16,2021, https://www.newsweek.com /number-us-soldiers-who-died-afghanistan-war-1619685.
9 – John F. Harris, Newsweek, October 15, 2001, https://www.washingtonpost.com/archive/politics/2001/10/15/bush-rejects-taliban-offer-on-bin-laden/bc0ec919-082b-40e6-91ca-55e5ca34a70a/.
10 – Islam Question & Answer, https://islamqa.info/en/answers/13998/verses-and-ahadith-about-hijab-in-islam.
11 – Daniel Brown, Task & Purpose Business Insider, November 9, 2018, https://taskandpurpose.com/news/afghanistan-iraq-death-toll/.

12 – Wikipedia, "United States Military Casualties of War",
   https://en.wikipedia.org/wiki/United_States _military_casualties_of_war.
13 – Kit Klarenberg, Mint Press News, "Files Expose Syrian 'Revolution' as
   Western Regime Change Operation, September 27, 2023
   https://www.mintpressnews.com/central-crisis-management-cell-files-
   expose-syria-western-regime-change/285803/.
14 – Whitney Webb, Mint Press News, "How the US Occupied the 30% of Syria,
   Containing Most of Its Oil, Water, and Gas", April 16, 2018,
   https://www.mintpressnews.com/how-the-us-occupied-the-30-of-syria-
   containing-most-of-its-oil-water-and-gas/240601/.
15 – David Brennan, Newsweek, January 15, 2020, https://www.newsweek.com
   /donald-trump-us-troops-syria-oil-bashar-al-assad-kurds-wisconsin-rally-
   1482250.
16 – Anchal Vohra, Foreign Policy, January 11, 2022, https://foreignpolicy.com/
   2022/01/11/syria-sanctions-america-biden-europe-economy/.
17 – Jonathan Bradley, Western Standard, January 11, 2023,
   https://www.westernstandard.news/news/snowden-says-the-cia-involved-in-
   pro-democracy-protests-worldwide/article_6a1eac6a-9108-11ed-85b8-
   3777167667f3.html.
18 – Charity & Security Network, August 30, 2016,
   https://www.theguardian.com/commentisfree/2015/jun/03/us-isis-syria-iraq.
19 – Seumas Milne, The Guardian, June 3, 2015, https://www.theguardian.com/
   commentisfree/2015/jun/03/us-isis-syria-iraq.
20 – Jon Jackson, Newsweek, March 3, 2022, https://www.newsweek.com/
   watch-madeleine-albright-saying-iraqi-kids-deaths-worth-it-resurfaces-
   1691193.
21 – Kent Klein, Voice of America, May 23, 2012,
   https://www.voanews.com/a/obama_tells_air_force_academy_us_is_one_i
   ndispensable_country_world_affairs/940158.html.
22 – Allan R. Millett, Britanica, https://www.britannica.com/event/Korean-War.
23 – CNN, "Korean War Fast Facts", July 21, 2023m https://edition.cnn.com/
   2013/06/28/world/asia/korean-war-fast-facts/index.html.
24 – John Harrington and Grant Suneson, USA Today, June 13 2019,
   https://www.usatoday.com/story/money/2019/06/13/cost-of-war-13-most-
   expensive-wars-in-us-history/39556983/
25 – National Archives, "U.S. Enters the Korean Conflict",
   https://www.archives.gov/education/lessons/korean-conflict.
26 – Sebastien Roblin, The National Interest, June 24, 2020,
   https://nationalinterest.org/blog/reboot/did-north-korea-really-start-korean-
   war-china-doesnt-think-so-163457.
27 – Tom Powell, Greanville Post, "War in Korea: Forgotten, Distorted
   Surpressed, Why?" February 15, 2024, https://www.greanvillepost.com/
   2024/02/15/war-in-korea-forgotten-distorted-supressed-why/
28 – Blaine Taylor, National History Network, https://warfarehistorynetwork.com/
   douglas-macarthur-atomic-bombs-will-win-the-korean-war/.
29 – Jesse Greenspan, History, August 29, 2018, https://www.history.com/news/
   8-things-you-should-know-about-the-korean-war.
30 – Ronald H. Spector, Britannica, March 1, 2024, https://www.britannica.com/
   event/Vietnam-War.
31 – John Harrington and Grant Suneson, USA Today, June 13 2019,
   https://www.usatoday.com/story/money/2019/06/13/cost-of-war-13-most-
   expensive-wars-in-us-history/39556983/

32 – Pangambam S, Sinju Press, May 16, 2016, https://singjupost.com/full-transcript-president-kennedys-peace-speech-at-american-university-june-10-1963/.

33 – Wikipedia, "Bay of Pigs Invasion", https://en.wikipedia.org/wiki/Bay_of_Pigs_Invasion.

34 – Wikipedia, "Cuban Missile Crisis", https://en.wikipedia.org/wiki/Cuban_Missile_Crisis.

35 – Jeffrey Sachs, Penguin Random House, *To Move the World: JFK's Quest for Peace,* https://www.penguinrandomhouse.com/books/227581/to-move-the-world-by-jeffrey-d-sachs/.

36 – Britannica, "Chinese Communist Party", March 3, 2024, https://www.britannica.com/topic/Chinese-Communist-Party.

37 – World Atlas, "What Type Of Government Does Laos Have?", https://www.worldatlas.com/articles/what-type-of-government-does-laos-have.html.

38 – Christopher Wolf and Elliot Davis Jr., U.S. News & World Report, February 23, 2024, https://www.usnews.com/news/best-countries/articles/2023-02-24/these-countries-have-sent-the-most-aid-to-ukraine.

39 – Brown University's Watson Institute Cost of War Project, "Millions displaced by U.S. post-9/11 wars", https://watson.brown.edu/costsofwar/files/cow/imce/papers/2021/Costs of War_Vine et al_Displacement Update August 2021.pdf.

40 – Brown University's Watson Institute Cost of War Project, "Human Cost of post-9/11 wars", https://watson.brown.edu/costsofwar/figures/2021/WarDeathToll.

41 – Brown University's Watson Institute Cost of War Project, "Estimate of U.S. post-911 War Spending, FY2001-2022", https://watson.brown.edu/costsofwar/ figures/2021/BudgetaryCosts.

State and Municipal Government Debt

1 – Official Website of Truth in Accounting. https://www.truthinaccounting.org/.

2 – Jennifer Ludden, NPR, https://www.npr.org/2023/09/12/1198923453/child-poverty-child-tax-credi-pandemic-aid-census-data.

3 – Brendan Weber, NBC Los Angeles, September 19, 2016, https://www.nbclosangeles.com/news/national-international/one-fifth-of-californians-living-in-poverty-report/110837/.

4 – World Population Review, https://worldpopulationreview.com/states.

5 – Paulina Cachero and Claire Ballentine, Bloomberg News, https://www.bloomberg.com/news/articles/2023-09-20/nearly-half-of-young-adults-are-living-back-home-with-parents?cmpid=BBD092023_BIZ.

6 – Elizabeth Napolitano, CBS News Moneywatch, September 21, 2023, https://www.cbsnews.com/news/gen-z-millennials-living-at-home-harris-poll/.

7 – Stephen H. Woolf, PBS, January 9, 2016, https://www.pbs.org/newshour/health/report-americans-less-healthy-die-younger-than-global-peers.

8 – Maggie Fox, NBC News, November 17, 2016, https://www.nbcnews.com/health/health-care/united-states-comes-last-again-health-compared-other-countries-n684851.

9 – Maria Hadaya, Optimed Hospitalists, "How Healthy Is America Compared to Other countries, March 24, 2022, https://optimeddoctors.com/how-healthy-is-america/.

10 – *Ibid,* https://optimeddoctors.com/how-healthy-is-america/.

11 – CDC, "Adult Obesity Facts", https://www.cdc.gov/obesity/data/adult.html.

12 – United Nations, "Universal Declaration of Human Rights", https://www.un.org/sites/un2.un.org/files/2021/03/udhr.pdf.

13 – Worldometer, https://www.worldometers.info/demographics/life-expectancy/.

14 – Michael Daniel, John Hopkins Medicine, May 3, 2016, https://www.hopkinsmedicine.org/news/media/releases/study_suggests_medical_errors_now_third_leading_cause_of_death_in_the_us.

15 – Centers for Disease Control and Prevention, "Suicide Data and Statistics", https://www.cdc.gov/suicide/suicide-data-statistics.html.

16 – Shem Gordon, Health, "Youth Suicide Rates Have Increased Over the Past Decade, Experts Push Crucial Changes", June 26, 2023, https://www.health.com/youth-suicide-rate-increase-cdc-report-7551663.

17 – Noah Weiland, New York Times, "U.S. Recorded Nearly 110,000 Overdose Deaths in 2022", May 17, 2023, https://www.nytimes.com/2023/05/17/us/politics/drug-overdose-deaths.html.

18 – Diedre McPhillips, CNN, May 18, 2023, https://edition.cnn.com/2023/05/18/health/drug-overdose-deaths-2022/index.html.

19 – Preeti Vankar, Statistica, January 24, 2024, https://www.statista.com/statistics/611017/drug-overdose-deaths-number-in-the-us-by-age/.

20 – WHYY PBS, March 8, 2013, https://whyy.org/articles/school-reform-commission-votes-to-close-23-philadelphia-schools/.

21 – Wikipedia, "List of closed public schools in Detroit, https://en.wikipedia.org/wiki/List_of_closed_public_schools_in_Detroit.

22 – Holly Peele and Maya Riser-Kositski, Education Week, "Corona Virus and School Closures in 2019-2020", https://www.edweek.org/leadership/map-coronavirus-and-school-closures-in-2019-2020/2020/03.

23 – Rachel M. Cohen, Alternet, "The Devastating Impact of School Closures on Students and Communities", April 18, 2016, https://www.alternet.org/2016/04/devastating-impact-school-closures-students-and-communities.

24 – National Center for Education Statistics, "Closed schools", https://nces.ed.gov/fastfacts/display.asp?id=619.

25 – John Rachel's personal blogsite, "When Hope Becomes Hype", May 25, 2014, https://jdrachel.com/2014/05/25/when-hope-becomes-hype/.

26 – Finances Online, "Countries with Free College Education", https://financesonline.com/free-college-education-statistics/.

27 – The Peace Dividend, Official Website. "Regime Change: Up Close and Personal", https://peacedividend.us/regime-change-up-close-and-personal/.

28 – Anna Helhoski and Eliza Haverstock, Nerdwallet, January 19, 2023, https://www.nerdwallet.com/article/loans/student-loans/how-many-americans-have-student-loan-debt.

29 – Alicia Hahn and Jordan Tarver, Forbes Advisor, June 16, 2023, https://www.forbes.com/advisor/student-loans/average-student-loan-debt-statistics/.

30 – Seth Baum, Federation of American Scientists, "The Risk of Nuclear Winter", May 29, 2015, https://fas.org/publication/risk-nuclear-winter/.

31 – Center for Arms Control and Non-Proliferation, "Fact Sheet: U.S. Nuclear Weapons Modernization: Cost and Constraints", January 22, 2021, https://armscontrolcenter.org/fact-sheet-u-s-nuclear-weapons-modernization-costs-constraints/32.

32 – U.S. Department of Housing and Urban Development, "The 2023 Annual Homelessness Assessment Report (AHAR) to Congress", https://www.huduser.gov/portal/sites/default/files/pdf/2023-AHAR-Part-1.pdf.

33 – National Alliance to End Homelessness", https://endhomelessness.org/homelessness-in-america/homelessness-statistics/state-of-homelessness/.

34 – USA Facts, May 16, 2023, https://usafacts.org/articles/which-states-have-the-highest-and-lowest-rates-of-homelessness/.

35 – *Ibid*, https://usafacts.org/articles/which-states-have-the-highest-and-lowest-rates-of-homelessness/.

36 – Katharina Buchholz, Statistica, March 7, 2023, https://www.statista.com/chart/6949/the-us-cities-with-the-most-homeless-people/.

37 – Brett Wilkens, Common Dreams, "UN Human Rights Body Issues 'Scathing' Report on Sweeping US Violations, November 3, 2023, https://www.commondreams.org/news/human-rights-united-states.

38 – Brenda Richardson, Forbes, March 7, 2022, https://www.forbes.com/sites/brendarichardson/2022/03/07/16-million-homes-lie-empty-and-these-states-are-the-vacancy-hot-spots/?sh=7ba0a5c327c1.

39 – Sami Adler, Global Giving, March 1, 2021, https://www.globalgiving.org/learn/how-much-would-it-cost-to-end-homelessness-in-america/

40 – Force Project, "How Much Is the Cost for Operational of Aircraft Carrier?", https://forcesproject.com/cost-for-operational-of-aircraft-carrier/.

Whose Money Is It Anyway?

1 – Wikipedia, "District of Columbia Organic Act of 1871". https://en.wikipedia.org/wiki/District_of_Columbia_Organic_Act_of_1871.

2 – Paul Krugman, New York Times, "America Isn't a Corporation", January 12, 2012, https://www.nytimes.com/2012/01/13/opinion/krugman-america-isnt-a-corporation.html.

3 – The Peace Dividend, Official Website. "The Peace Dividend Refund", https://peacedividend.us/the-peace-dividend/the-peace-dividend-refund/.

4 – The Peace Dividend, Official Website. "The Peace Dividend", https://peacedividend.us/the-peace-dividend/.

5 – The Peace Dividend, Official Website. "Electing a Peace Dividend Congress", https://peacedividend.us/the-peace-dividend/electing-a-peace-dividend-congress/.

Personal Debt

1 – The Zebra, "Home Ownership Statistics", January 31, 2023, https://www.thezebra.com/resources/research/homeownership-statistics/.

2 – Jacob Channel, Lending Tree, "Mortgage Statistics: 2024", November 30, 2023. https://www.lendingtree.com/home/mortgage/u-s-mortgage-market-statistics/.

3 – Statistica, https://www.statista.com/statistics/248289/home-mortgage-sector-debt-outstanding-in-the-united-states/.

4 – *Ibid*, https://www.lendingtree.com/home/mortgage/u-s-mortgage-market-statistics/.

5 – Alicia Wallace, CNN, November 7, 2023, https://edition.cnn.com/2023/11/07/ economy/household-debt-credit-card-delinquencies-q3/index.html.

6 – Michelle Black, Forbes Advisor, "Average Credit Card Debt Study", January 17, 2024, https://www.forbes.com/advisor/credit-cards/average-credit-card-debt/.

7 – US Inflation Calculator, "Current US Inflation Rates: 2000-2024", https://www.usinflationcalculator.com/inflation/current-inflation-rates/.

8 – *Ibid,* https://edition.cnn.com/2023/11/07/economy/household-debt-credit-card-delinquencies-q3/index.html.

9 – Statisitica, https://www.statista.com/statistics/453380/outstanding-automotive-loan-balances-usa/.

10 – Finmasters, https://finmasters.com/car-loan-statistics/.

11 – Antonio Pequeño IV, Forbes, October 21, 2023, https://www.forbes.com/sites/antoniopequenoiv/2023/10/21/americans-are-overdue-with-their-car-payments-at-highest-rate-in-nearly-30-years/?sh=796cf2833d04.

12 – Alicia Hahn and Jordan Tarver, Forbes Advisor, July 16, 2023, https://www.forbes.com/advisor/student-loans/average-student-loan-debt-statistics/.

13 – Emily Guy Birken and Ashley Harrison, USA Today, October 16, 2023, https://www.usatoday.com/money/blueprint/debt/average-american-debt-statistics/.

14 – *Ibid,* https://www.usatoday.com/money/blueprint/debt/average-american-debt-statistics/.

15 – Consumer Finance Protection Bureau, February 2022, https://files.consumerfinance.gov/f/documents/cfpb_medical-debt-burden-in-the-united-states_report_2022-03.pdf.

16 – Will Daniel, Fortune, May 24, 2023, https://fortune.com/2023/05/23/inflation-economy-consumer-finances-americans-cant-cover-emergency-expense-federal-reserve/.

17 – Priya Krishna, New York Times, "Eat Now, Pay Later: Going Into Debt for Food, August 29, 2022, https://www.nytimes.com/2022/08/29/dining/buy-now-pay-later-loans-groceries.html.

18 – Stephen Daggett, Congressional Research Service, "Cost of Major U.S. Wars", June 29, 2010, https://sgp.fas.org/crs/natsec/RS22926.pdf.

19 – *Ibid,* https://watson.brown.edu/costsofwar/figures/2021/BudgetaryCosts.

20 – Chris Lange, 24/7 Wall Street, November 14, 2023, https://247wallst.com/special-report/2023/11/14/us-military-spending-every-year-since-1970/.

21 – The National Military Strategy of the United States of America, https://history.defense.gov/Portals/70/Documents/nms/nms2004.pdf?ver=2014-06-25-123447-627.

The Systemic Poison Pill

1 – Hanna Ziady and Tammy Luhby, CNN, "US national debt hits record $34 trillion", January 3, 2024, https://edition.cnn.com/2024/01/03/economy/us-national-debt-34-trillion/index.html.

2 – Wikipedia, "Ponzi scheme", https://en.wikipedia.org/wiki/Ponzi_scheme.

3 – FRED Economic Data, St. Louis Fed, "Federal Debt as Held by Foreign and International Investors as Percent of Gross Domestic Product", https://fred.stlouisfed.org/series/HBFIGDQ188S.

4 – Ruth Carson and Mark Cudmore, Bloomberg, "US Debt Interest Bill Rockets Past a Cool $1 Trillion a Year", November 8, 2023, https://www.bloomberg.com/news/articles/2023-11-07/us-debt-bill-rockets-past-a-cool-1-trillion-a-year#xj4y7vzkg.

5 – Phil Rosen, Business Insider, "The Fed has a very strong case to keep interest rates higher for longer", February 17, 2024, https://www.businessinsider.com/recession-outlook-fed-interest-rate-cuts-wall-street-markets-investors-2024-2.

6 – Sputnik International, "A History of US Government Shutdowns", April 10, 2023, https://sputnikglobe.com/20231004/a-history-of-us-government-shutdowns-1113860745.html.

7 – Wikipedia, "Federal Reserve Act", https://en.wikipedia.org/wiki/Federal_Reserve_Act.

Peace Dollars: A Modest Beginning

1 – White Out Press, "Who Really Assassinated Abe Lincoln and John F. Kennedy", October 4, 2022, https://www.whiteoutpress.com/who-really-assassinated-abe-lincoln-and-john-f-kennedy583/.

2 – Staff of the Federal Reserve Bank of Kansas City, Federal Reserve History, "Federal Reserve Act Signed into Law, December 23, 1913", https://www.federalreservehistory.org/essays/federal-reserve-act-signed.

3 – David Bollier, Resilience, "Reclaiming Public Control of Money-Creation", September7, 2017, https://www.resilience.org/stories/2017-09-07/reclaiming-public-control-money-creation/.

Closing Editorial Comments

1 – Pew Research Center, "Inflation, Health Costs, Partisan Cooperation Among the Nation's Top Problems", June 21, 2023, https://www.pewresearch.org/politics/2023/06/21/inflation-health-costs-partisan-cooperation-among-the-nations-top-problems/.

About the Peace Dividend Project

As I hope I made explicitly clear, I believe military extravagance and the entire imperial project – establishing the U.S. as lord and master over the entire planet – is the "Achilles heel" of the establishment's hammerlock on our foreign and domestic policy-making apparatus. The excesses are so extreme and so obvious, they offer on a silver platter the big wakeup call we need to get everyday Americans on board with regime change in Washington DC.

America's overt, aggressively pursued goal of global empire is operating at full throttle. Regardless of how the current conflict in Ukraine is resolved, this hegemonic campaign will continue unless we the people put an end to the ambitious but suicidal enterprise. It certainly will not stop itself. Nor will anyone currently in power stop it. The incessant prattling we hear about WWIII and nuclear war is not idle talk. It's preparing the public for what's to come.

We obviously are hoping the Peace Dividend strategy will be immediately and fully implemented. Much-needed relief will begin flowing to U.S. citizens in the form of Peace Dividend refund checks. More importantly, the trajectory of perpetual war and infinite military expansion will be halted and reversed.

This requires a vast mobilization. It's an epic struggle for a future which reflects the best of our people and offers real hope. At the same time, we must be realistic. It might take time.

While our struggle for a peaceful world unfolds, the colossal military expenditures continue to mount. This means that the total dollar amount of the waste and the size of the Peace Dividend refund will continue to increase.

For updates, please go to the official Peace Dividend website …

https://peacedividend.us

Related Books by John Rachel

If you found this book informative and interesting, please
consider these titles by this same author.

*A powerful and empowering collection of
commentaries and insights by some of today's
most respected political thinkers. Perpetual war
is destroying our nation. To stop the unfolding
disaster, we must honestly look at how our own
leadership and policies have led the country astray.
This book is the perfect place to start.*

Amazon (Kindle): bit.ly/3YSF0OP
Amazon (Print): bit.ly/3qNuqfn
Direct from printer: bit.ly/3PcTJRr
Barnes & Noble: bit.ly/3PcLTXZ
Apple iBook: bit.ly/3QQqC7K
Smashwords: bit.ly/3EePWgk

*For there to be any progress, for everyday citizens
to have a voice in shaping the future they want for
themselves and future generations, we must elect a
congress that truly represents and serves the people!
If you embrace what Robert F. Kennedy Jr. has
been saying in his presidential campaign, that
equates to electing a Kennedy congress!*

Amazon (Kindle): bit.ly/49CvDHP
Amazon (Print): bit.ly/3QMjlV0
Direct from printer: bit.ly/3FYYx7v
Barnes & Noble: bit.ly/46daAJe
Apple iBook: bit.ly/3SGeRBy
Smashwords: bit.ly/3uhwg9P
Kobo: bit.ly/3SA7jR0

The Peace Dividend strategy is a direct attack on America's systemic addiction to war by appealing to the self-interest of its citizens. The Peace Dividend concept literally INCENTIVIZES citizens to redirect their thinking and start WORKING FOR PEACE! This short book explains how we put America back on a path of peace and prosperity.

Amazon (Kindle): amzn.to/2cpIRfQ
Amazon (Print): amzn.to/2cEhnCb
Direct from printer: bit.ly/2c3mJsl
Barnes & Noble: bit.ly/2cWxvzd
Apple iBook: apple.co/2cqw7an
Smashwords: bit.ly/2cb6Cse

Prepare to see the future of American democracy! This manifesto offers a detailed, step-by-step plan for cleaning up the corruption in Washington DC. This is electoral reform so radical that in one master stroke it puts America on the path to a healthy economy and directly addresses its #1 and #2 challenges: the suicidal march to war and the destructive impact of a historically high level of wealth inequality.

Amazon (Kindle): amzn.to/1QJRiNZ
Amazon (Print): amzn.to/1Cuq0du
Barnes & Noble: bit.ly/1GpTTLq
Apple iBook: apple.co/1BXnPcy
Smashwords: bit.ly/1B4DQCp
Kobo: bit.ly/1QETE64

This is a manual for constructive voting in the 2016 election. It presents a concrete plan for wresting control of the country and our democracy back from the rich and powerful and restoring the constitutional mandate of government of the people, by the people, and for the people. It's not just more whining. It's a real plan!

Amazon (Kindle): amzn.to/1VMf2Ft
Amazon (Print): amzn.to/1L9SdIC
Direct from printer: bit.ly/1i7ISFM
Amazon CA: amzn.to/1in513n
Amazon GB: amzn.to/1KfjtQO
Amazon JP: amzn.to/1OMslBG

In this political drama, a bright, young, idealistic, Green Party candidate in his bid for the congressional seat of a conservative district in Ohio, teams with a beautiful, fiery African-American intern to combat the slick deceptions and ruthless tactics of a sweet-talking right wing incumbent.

Amazon (Kindle): amzn.to/1jetpiY
Amazon (Print): amzn.to/1lddvsp
Barnes & Noble: bit.ly/1l5FmuG
Apple iBook: bit.ly/1gT2O7w
Smashwords: bit.ly/1fIU3Mq

Coming Soon!

[The Art of War: The Science of Peace]

About the Author

John Rachel has a B.A. in Philosophy, is a novelist and established political blogger. He has written ten novels, five political and two creative non-fiction books. His political articles have appeared at Nation of Change, Counterpunch, Dissident Voice, Popular Resistance, OpEdNews, Greanville Post, and other alternative media outlets.

He heads up the Peace Dividend Project and is the creator of the CFAR (Contract for American Renewal) electoral reform strategy.

Since leaving the U.S. in 2006, he has lived in and explored 34 countries. He now permanently resides in a traditional, rural Japanese community about an hour from Osaka, where he lives with his wife of twelve years. Daily he rides his bicycle through the soybean fields and rice paddies of the surrounding landscape and experiences infinite delight in the ringing of temple bells three times a day by monks at a local Shinto shrine. These days he is mostly immersed in good vibrations.

You can follow his writing and evolution of his world view at:

https://jdrachel.com

Acknowledgements

For over eleven years now, peace and electoral reform have been the focus of my political activism and writing. Neither have been satisfying or promising pursuits. Resistance to new ideas, even among those who claim to be devoted to promoting a peaceful world and true representative democracy, is endemic. Rationalizations and twisted logic rule, as with the "leftists" who myopically buy into the neocon fraud that fighting the Russians in Ukraine is supporting the spread of democratic ideals and opposing megalomaniac tyranny. It's difficult, if not entirely impossible, to have a rational discussion with people who have no grasp of history, are completely misinformed — a polite way of saying 'brainwashed' — are too preoccupied with tribal loyalty to look at facts and are incapable of objective and balanced analysis. This cerebral anechoic chamber is further shackled by stubborn adherence by activists to legacy methods and tactics, and an antiquated view of the mechanisms of political power. Most current activists, especially in the peace movement, tragically are stuck in the early 70s, while the rest of the world has moved on.

Even so, I've refused to give up pushing my outside-the-box ideas to the deaf, dumb and blind. I wonder if that just means I unconditionally fail Einstein's sanity test.

Through the adversity and setbacks which have populated my best attempts at communicating and working with the remnants of a progressive left, my lovely Japanese wife has remained steadfast in her encouragement and support. Her tempered but timely praise for my persistence and determination has helped immeasurably. For this I am infinitely grateful.

I also must credit those individuals who have given me the inspiration to do what I do. These immediately come to mind: Lord Bertrand Russell, Henry Wallace, President John F. Kennedy, Robert F. Kennedy, George McGovern, Paul Wellstone, Jimmy Carter, Ron Paul, Mike Gravel, Daniel Ellsberg, Ralph Nader, Julian Assange, and Edward Snowden.

What certainly comes through loud and clear from those who advocate peace and dare to speak truth to power, is the need for some profound changes in the way the U.S. conducts itself in the world. Let this be a beginning at building a nation and society we can embrace with pride and humility, then confidently and proudly hand off to our children.

Legal Notices and Disclaimers

John Rachel's Personal Website

Peace Dividend Website

No Contract No Vote Website